JPM PUBLICATIONS

Contents

This Way Mexico

Ancient Heritage

A crossroads of fabulous cultures, Mexico stands out as a country where history and legend intertwine. When the Spanish conquistadors first set foot in central America in 1521, they encountered a land where successive civilizations had been thriving for some 3000 years.

The first foundations had been laid by the Olmecs. The Teotihuacán civilization established a resolutely urban society. They were followed by the Maya, remarkable astronomers, then came the Toltecs and, finally, the Aztecs. The proud symbol emblazoned on the Mexican flag—an eagle perched on a cactus, with a snake in its beak—recalls those ancient times. According to tradition, a serpent-eating eagle had shown the Aztecs the spot where they should establish their capital, Tenochtitlán—a city later described by an awed Hernán Cortés as "the most beautiful in the world". It was to become the centre of a huge empire.

Then came the shock of European conquest. Even during the long period of colonization, Mexico's ancient legacy was never buried too deeply beneath the surface layer of "Spanishness". Today Mexico is a nation which has rediscovered its past, a rich heritage illustrated by more than 10,000 archaeological sites scattered throughout the country. The chance discovery in the 18th century of the famous Aztec "Sun Stone", under the main square in Mexico City, marked the beginning of Mexico's fascination for its historical roots, a process which has inspired a new national awareness.

The Mexican Identity

Over the centuries, the fusion of pre-Columbian heritage and Iberian society produced a unique nation. The Iberian and Indian personalities were not so unalike, after all. Their religious beliefs were radically different, and the Spanish conquest brought bloody battles, but the two peoples shared a similar attitude: a strong sense of pride, a pugnacious temperament, an inclination to show off, and an autocratic political system. These common elements shaped the character of a nation that was ultimately neither Indian nor Spanish, but Mexican. This identity is embodied in a number of qualities: national pride, faultless hospitality, devotion to the family, religious fervour.

A stone mask in the Temple of Quetzalcóatl in Teotihuacán depicts Tláloc, the rain god.

The Mexican attitude towards religion is perhaps the most dramatic example of this dual heritage. In the rural areas, religious beliefs are a combination of pre-Columbian rites and Christian practices. The Virgin of Guadalupe, the patron saint of Mexico, is none other than Tonantzín, the earth goddess. Quetzalcóatl, her son, comfortably assumes the personality of Jesus Christ. It is during the popular fiestas—of which there are more than 4,300 throughout the year—that folk mysticism reaches its greatest heights. The fun and celebrations are but a superficial expression of profound religious zeal, as seen, for example, during the Feast of All Saints, with its strong symbolism of Life and Death.

Indian Country

In Mexico, 56 different Indian groups, around 10 per cent of the population, have maintained their own language. Their territories sometimes coincide with the ancient pre-Columbian empires, but many other groups, refusing the domination of the conquering Spaniards, were forced to take refuge in less accessible regions. This enabled them to keep their culture virtually intact. The lifestyle of some tribes is not unlike that of the pre-Columbian days, based on self-sufficiency, with the cultivation of corn (maize) as its mainstay.

There are three major Indian regions. The central one, near Mexico City, is home to the descendants of the Náhuatl-speaking Aztecs and their dependent peoples, the Tarasco of Michoacán, the Mixtecs and Zapotecs. Descendants of the Maya are concentrated in the southeast, close to the frontier with Guatemala. The wild northern territory encompasses the old Chichimec region. The name, an Aztec term, designates the "barbarian" tribes of the steppes, the Cora and Huichol, Yaqui and Tarahumaras.

The independent existence of the Indians was achieved through bloodshed—the last Indian revolts took place at the end of the 19th century—and it is only with much perseverance that you will have a chance to become more closely acquainted with these living witnesses of Mexico's ancient splendour.

Land of the Gods

Sprawling over Mexico's central plateau at an altitude of 2,250 m (7,380 ft), Mexico City is the most populous capital in the world, with 21 million inhabitants at the last count. The country, nearly 2 million sq km (772,000 sq miles) in area, is the third largest in Latin America. In terms of population it's the second-largest, with nearly 100 million inhabitants.

The Tropic of Cancer cuts the country almost into two halves. The southern regions turn towards tropical Central America, while the north is firmly attached to the North American continent. This is the Mexico of westerns, a land of desert and cacti, reaching as far as the long, sun-baked peninsula of Baja California.

The Sierra Madre forms the country's backbone, enclosing between its eastern and western chains the highlands of the Altiplano. Most of the large cities are located here. The highlands are bordered to the south by the towering snow-capped volcanic peaks of Orizaba, 5700 m (18,700 ft) and Popocatéptl, 5,452 m (17,886 ft), reminders of the violent geological movements that periodically shake the land. The sometimes vertiginous slopes of the Altiplano loom over plains that sweep to the Gulf of Mexico to the east and the Pacific Ocean to the west. Crops are grown on terraces, and together with mineral wealth, have made the region the veritable heart of the country.

To the south, the tropical forest starts at the isthmus of Tehuantepec, linking the limestone expanse of the Yucatán peninsula and mountainous Chiapas with the rest of Mexico.

Flashback

From the Origins to the Olmecs

During the Upper Palaeolithic period (20,000–15,000 BC), nomadic tribes from northern Asia migrated across the Bering Strait to explore the virgin lands of America. These peoples gradually fanned out across the entire continent.

The territory that makes up present-day Mexico was settled around 5000–4000 BC, about the same time as the appearance of agriculture. The cultivation of corn, which was to become the staple food of future Meso-American civilizations, was of capital importance. Around 1150 BC, larger communities were founded along the Tierras Calientes ("warm lands") of the Gulf of Mexico. San Lorenzo was the first large Olmec town.

The principal centres seem to have developed around specific resources: San Lorenzo had rich supplies of clay used for pottery; La Venta exploited salt, tar and rubber; Laguna de los Ceros and Tres Zapotes governed access to the basalt quarries which provided the building materials for some of Mexico's most famous monuments. The Olmecs are best known for sculpting gigantic heads of stone. Carved between 1200 and 900 BC, they represent important personalities, perhaps warriors, but more probably the *caciques*, or tribal chiefs. The biggest one found weighs more than 40 tonnes.

The cities had a rigid social structure, dominated by a handful of individuals who held the reins of power. The complex Olmec society nurtured many features of the future civilizations—they invented a theory of the origin of the universe, played ball games and performed ritual sacrifice. Cultural development and the progressive expansion of their trade network carried the Olmec influence to the four corners of Meso-America, to the point that some researchers are now questioning whether the region of the gulf was indeed their homeland.

Around 400 BC the Olmec civilization suddenly collapsed, perhaps after a revolt. But eight centuries of Olmec dominion left a number of achievements which make it the mother of all Central American cultures.

Aztec life before Cortés, depicted by Diego Rivera in Mexico City's National Palace.

Teotihuacán

By 300 BC, a sedentary lifestyle had spread to all of central and southern Mexico. The Zapotec built a city of 20,000 at Monte Albán, and began to use a calendar with hieroglyphic numbers.

But the first real urban centre of the continent developed in the central highlands: Teotihuacán, the "City of the Gods", as the Aztecs would later call it. Founded at the beginning of the Christian era, the city was built to an astrological plan. It spread over more than 20 sq km (7.7 sq miles), and by the 2nd century already had a population of at least 50,000, perhaps twice as many. Among its monuments were the Pyramid of the Sun and the Pyramid of the Moon. Ideally located at the confluence of trade routes and close to obsidian quarries, Teotihuacán experienced a period of great prosperity up to end of the 5th century, growing to a metropolis of perhaps 200,000 inhabitants. At its height, it could have rivalled Rome in size and splendour. The economic, political, and ideological authority of the Teotihuacán nation was felt even in Maya country. We know nothing of the language or the origin of the city's founders, but numerous traces confirm the existence of a highly structured society in which traders and craftsmen enjoyed a special status.

Then, abruptly, and for no known reason, Teotihuacán foundered. Several hypotheses have been suggested: a popular uprising, invasion, epidemic, overpopulation, and so on. By 750, the first great city of Central America was nothing more than a pile of rubble, while the neighbouring towns of Cholula and Xochicalco gained in strength.

Maya Culture

The Maya lands are historically divided into three regions: the Guatemala highlands where the main communities were established at Kaminaljuyú (500–200 BC) and the Pacific coast (Izapa, 200 BC–AD 200); the central forest of Petén; and the Yucatec peninsula to the north. The foundations of what was to become one of the most brilliant civilizations were laid, to flourish finally at Tikal, in the low country of Petén. It was the start of what is known as the Classic period. The city was laid out around a plaza surrounded by pyramids and smaller buildings, referred to as "palaces". This kernel formed the ceremonial centre but was also the city proper, enclosed by a wide boundary.

From AD 600, finally free of Teotihuacán imperialism, numerous regional capitals developed at Copán (Honduras), Palenque and, it seems, Calakmul. This was not a centralized empire, but rather a network of rival city states which shared the same basic culture. Competition favoured the rise of unprecedented activity in arts and crafts, best represented by stelae (carved stone slabs) and jade objects. The Maya developed an amazingly precise calendar and a complex writing system.

Antagonism between the different city states sparked numerous wars and probably led to their ultimate decline. Towards the end of the 8th century, these conflicts took a turn for the worse and trade discontinued. Around 850, the people migrated northwards in mass, leaving their cities to the encroaching jungle.

The Maya civilization lingered on in the Yucatán. Edzná, in the Chenes region, and the cities of the Puuc country, centred around Uxmal, developed their own architectural style. However, by the end of the 10th century, the area had come under Toltec rule.

The Toltec

After the decline of Teotihuacán, central Mexico was split up into city states. Only one of them, Tula, made an attempt to centralize power. Piecing together myth and reality, it would appear that the city had a population of around 35,000 in the 10th century. At first the principal deity was Quetzalcóatl, the Feathered Serpent, but he and his adepts were gradually dislodged by the Tezcatlipoca, a new, bloodthirsty warrior-god. Human sacrifices increased.

The influence of Tula grew rapidly, extending to the Yucatán, where the Toltec imposed their architecture and gods on the descendants of the Maya. The great city of Chichén Itzá was tied down in an alliance with Uxmal and Mayapán—the last major centre in this region.

Towards the end of the 12th century, bearing the brunt of invasions by the Chichimecs ("barbarians") from the north, Tula fell and its people were scattered. Yet, without realising it, they left a time bomb for these newcomers, in the form of a legend which was to bring about their downfall.

The Aztecs

At the beginning of the 14th century, immigrants arrived from a mythical place to the north called Aztlán. These Aztecs settled on the islands of Lake Texcoco, after witnessing the omen predicted by their principal deity, Huitzilopochtli: an eagle perched on a cactus, with a snake in its beak.

In spite of a chilly reception from the neighbouring tribes, the Aztecs (who renamed themselves Mexicas), first built a village, then a city: Tenochtitlán. Lacking space, they reclaimed it from the lake. Around 1426, they rebelled against the authority of the city state of Azcapotzalco, which held sway over the shores. At the head of a three-way alliance with the nearby cities of Texcoco and Tlacopán, they embarked on the conquest of the Mexico Basin, eventually controlling the entire centre of the country. The Totonac, the Mixtec and even the descendants of the Maya paid them tribute.

Mexica society, dominated by a feudal aristocracy, was subjected to the influence of the high priest Tlacaétel. More than 1,600 gods were worshipped, and the priests demanded ever-increasing numbers of human sacrifices. The Aztecs believed they lived in the last of five worlds: they held that only the blood of men, their most precious possession, could give the sun the strength to reappear every morning. In 1487, for the inauguration of the temple devoted to the sun god Huitzilopochtli, more than 20,000 human hearts were offered (some say 80,000!). The priests replenished their stock of prisoners during ritual "Wars of the Flowers" waged on neighbouring cities. However, not all the sacrificial victims were unwilling. Many welcomed their gruesome fate, convinced that they would rise to take their place beside the sun.

Though the Aztecs are remembered especially for their cruelty, they also had the gift of artistic genius. As heirs of all the civilizations that had preceded them, their culture was the synthesis of the knowledge and beliefs of the Meso-American world.

By the dawn of the 15th century, the Aztec empire knew no equal. With 250,000 inhabitants, their capital was one of the biggest and most beautiful cities in the world. Yet the foundations of the empire were insecure, worn down by constant warfare and a people increasingly weary of so many sacrifices. Its ruler Montezuma II was a sovereign of the divine order, himself burdened down by the weight of the ancient myths. And the evil omens were increasing. As spiritual heirs of the Toltecs, the Aztecs remembered the legend of Quetzalcóatl, who had long ago been driven from Tula: it had been predicted that during a "year of one reed" by the Mexica calendar, the god would return to reclaim his kingdom. That's when Hernán Cortés sailed into sight.

Birth of New Spain

Finding a new route to the Indies was the great craze in Europe at the end of the 15th century. Spain looked to the west to seek an economic revival. In 1517, 25 years after the landing of Columbus, the coast of Yucatán was reconnoitred by Spanish adventurers.

In 1518, Juan de Grijalva explored the shores of the Gulf of Mexico. It was in the following year, with the arrival of Cortés, that the history of modern Mexico began.

In spite of the opposition of the Viceroy of Cuba, who wanted to relieve him as commander of the expedition, Cortés set sail at the beginning of 1519 with 11 ships, over 500 men and 17 horses. After a short stop on the island of Cozumel, the conquistador disembarked on the Tabasco coast. A first skirmish with Maya warriors delivered him an Aztec slave, Malinche, who would become his mistress and interpreter. The Spaniards then landed at the site of today's Veracruz. News reached Montezuma of "floating mountains" transporting bearded white men. There was no doubt about it: Quetzalcóatl had returned. An embassy was despatched to meet the newcomers, but the magnificence of the entourage merely served to whet the Spaniards' appetite for gold.

Cortés received a warm welcome in Zempoala and quickly became aware of the local chiefs' hostility towards the Aztecs. On the road to Tenochtitlán, after a few initial clashes, the Spaniards made peace with the Tlaxcalecs and enlisted their aid. In November Cortés reached the Aztec capital with 6,000 allied warriors. The Spaniards were dazzled by the city. A rather reluctant Montezuma admitted the strange visitors, who were treated like gods, but Cortés, mistrustful of the Aztecs' intentions, held the emperor hostage in his own palace. When a Spanish expeditionary force landed at Veracruz to relieve Cortés of his command, he departed from Tenochtitlán, leaving his lieutenant Alvarado in charge.

In May 1520, Alvarado, fearing an attack, had 200 Aztec nobles massacred. When a victorious Cortés returned in June, it was to find his troops under siege. Montezuma, attempting to mediate, was stoned by the crowd. His successors refused to co-operate with the Spaniards, who decided to retreat from the city, sustaining heavy losses during the Noche Triste—the "Sad Night". Even so Cortés was not willing to give up. He mustered his forces and with the aid of 100,000 Tlaxcalecs laid siege to Tenochtitlán in May 1521. Less than three months later, the city fell.

Colonial Mexico

Mexico arose from the ashes of the defeated Aztec capital. New Spain was quickly organized, the conquered territory divided into *encomiendas* and distributed among the soldiers. Franciscan monks, and later Dominicans, arrived and baptised the Indians *en masse*. Temples were razed, idols destroyed. In their stead, abbeys and churches were built, and the Inquisition was introduced. Along with their religion, the Spaniards brought diseases unfamiliar to the Indians, and sickness was rampant.

Cortés was forced to surrender authority to a five-member *Audiencia*, which governed the country in a feudal manner. He and other Spanish conquistadors devoted themselves to further conquests. The myth of Eldorado led them ever further—to the Yucatán (taken in 1542), to Guatemala and the northern desert. In 1550 the discovery of rich silver deposits quickened the pace of the so-called "pacification". Acapulco became the centre for commerce with Asia, while Veracruz was the hub for trade with the Iberian peninsula. By the 18th century, the colony's mines were producing 11,000 tonnes of silver a year.

Coinciding with the decline of Spain, Mexico's society gradually stagnated. An urban minority held all the key posts, to the detriment of the Creoles (Spaniards born in Mexico). The Church became shamelessly rich: it owned half the country by the beginning of the 19th century. Carlos III of Spain tried to promote reform. The Jesuits were thrown out, and the ports were opened to foreign ships. The ideals of the American and French revolutions started to percolate through Mexican society. When Napoleon invaded Spain in 1808, the mother country was thrown into chaos, and aspirations of independence began to gather force in her American colonies.

Independence and Republic

On September 15, 1810, Father Miguel Hidalgo, a parish priest, launched his famous "Grito de Dolores" (Cry of Dolores), a call to revolt against Spain. It sparked a civil war which was to last 11 years. The movement originated with the well-to-do Creoles, but even they were quickly overwhelmed by its extent. Indians and mixed-race *mestizos* took up the cause and captured several towns in surprise attacks. Slavery was abolished in the liberated territories. But in the summer of 1811, Hidalgo, abandoned by his followers, was captured and executed. Another village priest, José María Morelos, took his place. Mexico City came under threat, Acapulco fell. Independence was proclaimed November 6, 1813, and a constitution was drafted in October the following year. However, when Morelos, too, was

A plume of smoke billows from the top of Popocatépetl volcano.

killed, the divisions between the various guerrilla chiefs spelled the end of the rebellion.

In the end, Mexico achieved only a watered-down emancipation: the conservatives, wary of the liberal tide that was sweeping Spain, allied themselves with the independent cause in order to secure their possessions. Independence was decreed on August 24, 1821. Nine months later, General Iturbide proclaimed himself Emperor of Mexico. but only two years elapsed before he was executed. General Antonio Lopez de Santa Anna entered on the scene with the first of a series of *pronunciamientos* (coups d'état) that returned him to power eleven times. The presidency changed hands 36 times in 22 years!

In 1836, American colonists who had settled in Texas, then a part of Mexico, proclaimed their own independence. Santa Anna was defeated and forced to retire. Ten years later, Texas joined the United States and Mexico declared war, but it lasted under a year and ended with Mexico's defeat. At the beginning of 1847, an American military expedition captured Mexico City itself. The 1848 Treaty of Guadalupe confirmed the loss of Texas and also ceded the provinces of upper California and New Mexico to the US—more than half of the Mexican territory.

Maximilian

During the 12 years following the departure of the Americans, Mexico was in the throes of civil war, as liberals and conservatives clashed with unmitigated violence. In 1861, Benito Juárez finally led the liberals to victory.

The country was bankrupt, and Juárez suspended payment of the foreign debt, leading to the intervention of its three major creditors. Spain, France and Britain sent an expeditionary force to collect their dues. Spain and Britain withdrew, but Napoleon III's France, fuelled by dreams of grandeur and territorial expansion, undertook the conquest of Mexico. The French emperor decided to entrust the throne to the Habsburg Archduke Maximilian, who took over his new post in June 1864. Believing he could reconcile the liberal Juaristas and the clergy, he was soon bogged down in the country's financial problems. When the US threw its support behind Juárez, Maximilian sent his wife Carlota to Europe to seek help. But Napoleon III, alarmed at the financial cost, made a volte-face. Forsaken by his allies, Maximilian was shot in June 1867.

Porfiriato

With Juárez back in power, the victory of the anti-clericals was complete. He tried to steer the country towards social reform but died in 1872. Porfirio Díaz, an old hero from the wars against the French, assumed power by championing non-re-eligibility, but ironically, he established himself as dictator and remained in power until 1911. During his regime, Mexico enjoyed a stable economic climate. However, the living conditions of the peasants were hardly better than those of slaves. At the beginning of the 20th century, 22 million ha (54 million acres) were owned by only eight individuals.

Revolution

In 1910 a wealthy Creole idealist, Francisco Madero, challenged Diaz for the presidency. He was imprisoned and later fled into exile. The north of the country rebelled, headed by Pancho Villa. In the south the revolution was led by Emiliano Zapata. On May 20, 1911, a truce was signed and Madero was chosen as president, but internal strife weakened his position. Zapata took up arms once again. Then the army chief, General Victoriano Huerta, betrayed Madero, had him shot and installed a repressive dictatorship.

Still, the flame of Revolution was rekindled. Headed by Venustiano Carranza, the insurgents gradually reconquered the entire country. In July 1914, Huerta fled, but peace for Mexico would still have to wait, as the different factions feuded, pitting Carranza and Alvaro Obregón against Villa and Zapata. At the beginning of 1916, Carranza was in power and a new social constitution was adopted though it was never really applied. Zapata was murdered in 1919; corruption was rampant. In a final jolt, Obregón was made president.

Modern Mexico

Under Obregón, the rebuilding of Mexico began. Various attempted coups were crushed. Plutarco Calles founded the Mexican Revolution Party, a single political body which was to evolve into the Institutional Revolutionary Party (PRI), still in power today. Sweeping social measures were gradually introduced: President Lázaro Cárdenas undertook the task of redistributing land to the peasants. In 1938, he nationalized the oil industry, risking a serious confrontation with the US.

Recent history is marked by rapid industrialization, largely financed by Mexico's petroleum resources. By the end of the 1970s, Mexico had become the fourth biggest oil producer in the world, but with the fall of the stock market around 1980 the country, indebted to the tune of $100 billion, entered an extreme economic crisis from which it has not yet recovered.

On the Scene

Like many other capitals, you could say that Mexico City is not really representative of Mexico. Or quite the opposite, that it embodies all of Mexico. This sprawling metropolis certainly has its own raison d'être and its own view of the world. But it's undeniable that here you can sense influences from all over the country, and traces of every period in its history.

MEXICO CITY

Zócalo, Alameda, Paseo de la Reforma, Chapultepec Park, Other Districts

The Aztecs, like the people of Athens or Rome, were proud to live in what they regarded as the most beautiful city in the world. Founded in 1325, Tenochtitlán was, at the time of the European conquest, at the pinnacle of its splendour. According to some accounts, almost half a million people dwelled in this floating city, in the middle of a lagoon. Anchored to the shore by three paved roads, criss-crossed by streets, avenues and canals, it dazzled the conquistadors. In size and power, it symbolized the might of the Aztec nation. The siege of 1521 left but a heap of ruins: Cortés wanted a clean slate to start building *his* capital.

Even today, Mexico City embodies political centralization. From the Aztecs to the Spanish then to modern times, it has always been the head and the heart of the country. Its magnetic pull has turned it into the biggest city in the world. Every day, 2,000 to 3,000 "parachutists"—as new arrivals are called—come here in search of a better life. By the beginning of 1996, Mexico had a population of 21 million *Chilangos*, and spread over more than 1000 sq km (385 sq miles).

Mexico City is frenzied, bewildering, electrifying, choked with traffic jams. Its streets teem with hawkers, obliged to find a means

The Concherías don feathers for the fiesta in honour of the Virgin of Guadalupe.

Jardín de San Fernando
San Hipólito
Paseo de la Reforma
Puente de Alvarado
Hotel Cortés
Hidalgo
Badillo
Casa de Castera
San Juan de Dios
V. Trujano
Mina
Pensador Mexicano
Sta Veracruz
Sta Veracruz
Av. Hidalgo
Av. Lázaro Cárdenas Norte
San Lorenzo
La Concepción
Cda. del 57
Rep. de
Museo Nacional de Arte
Museo Franz Meyer
Bellas Artes
Marconi
Xicoténcatl
Senad
Pinacoteca Virreinal
Mural Diego Rivera
Colón
Dr. Mora
Alameda
Jardín de la Solidaridad
Pal. Bellas Artes
Condesa
Pal. de Minería
Filomeno Mata
Betlemitas
La Opera
Av. Juárez
Casa de los Azulejos
5 de Mayo
Museo de Artes e Industrias Populares
Corpus Christi
Torre Latinoamericano
Fco. 1. Madero
San Francisco
Gante
Palacio de Iturbide
Humboldt
Revillagigedo
Independencia
Juárez
Casa de Castera
Dolores
16 de Septiembre
Articulo 123
Victoria
Cap. San Antonio
Sta. Maria de la Caridad
Venustiano Carranz
Plaza de Niñ
Ayuntamiento
San José
Rep. de Uruguay
Balderas
Casa Uluapa
Pescaditos
Plaza Carlos Pacheco
Mercado
Plaza de San Juan
Rep. del Salvador
E. Pugibet
S. Márquez
Bolívar
San Fe Neri
Mesones
Colegio de las Vizcaínas
Luis Moya
Delicias
Buentono
Aranda
López
San Ignacio
Aldaco
Eje. Lázaro Cárdenas Sur
dadela
Balderas
Arcos de Belén
Esperanza
Regina
Plaza Comercio
N. Sra. de Mercedítas
Plaza Cap. Malpica
Salto del Agua
Purísima Concepción
Salto del Agua
Igualdad
Nezahualcóy
N
0
500 m
0
500 yd

MEXICO CITY
HISTORIC CENTRE
Rep. Bolivia
Santo Domingo
Rep. de Brasil
Rep. de Argentina
ex-Pal. Sta Inquisición
La Expiración
Rep. de Colombia
Cjón. de Girón
Vicario
Plaza Santo Domingo
Ex-Real Aduana
La Encarnación
Rep de Venezuela
Rep. de Chile
González Obrégon
Casa Mayorazgo
Sta Catarina de Sena
Carmen
Loreto
Gral. M. Alemán
ex-Col. San Gregorio
La Enseñanza Antigua
San Ildefonso
ex-Col. San Ildefonso
Leona
Rodríguez Puebla
Casa Heras y Soto
Casa Conde del Apartado
Loreto Plaza
Sta Teresa La Nueva
Casa Vallarta
Monte de Piedad
Justo Sierra
Las Ajaracas
Mixcalco
Palma
Templo Mayor
Rep. de Guatemala
Catedral Metropolitana
Nac.Monte de Piedad
Sta Teresa la Antigua
Plaza de la Santisima
Sagrario
Arzobispado
La Profesa
Sta Inés
Santisima Trinidad
Margil
Moneda
Seminario
E. Zapata
Acad. San Carlos
Casa Miravelle
Plaza de la Constitución
Museo Nacional de las Culturas
Palacio Nacional
Soledad
Zócalo
Santisima
Jesús María
Casa San Mateo de Valparaíso
Museo Juárez
Col. de Todos Santos
Loreto
Alhóndiga
Ayuntamiento
Corregidora
Suprema Corte
5 de Febrero
Correo Mayor
San Bernardo
Porta Coeli
Manzanares
Talavera Alhóndiga
Pino Suárez
Plaza G. Bravo
San Agustín
Valvanera
Las Cruces
La Merced
Museo de la Ciudad de México
20 de Noviembre
Jesús Nazareno
Jesús María
Hosp. de Jesús
San José de Gracia
Roldán
Sto. Tomás
Misioneros
San Miguel
San Pablo el Nuevo
sé María Izazaga
Pino Suárez
San Pablo
Plaza San Pablo
Adoratorio Azteca
San Pablo el Viejo
Carretones
Topacio

of survival. Employment, housing and social services cannot keep pace with the rate of growth. Moreover, the city is sinking: the bed of Lake Texcoco on which it was built has sagged more than 7 m (23 ft) in 30 years because of over-exploitation of the ground water.

Mexico City is foundering, but there's still hope. The Chilangos are born optimists. They may be right. Perhaps the city's problems add to its appeal—a sort of Venice, condemned to vanish beneath the waves. The "palace city" described by the explorer Alexander von Humboldt at the beginning of the 19th century still exists. Every district retains the flavour of the old villages that it swallowed up. It won't be long until Mexico City counts 30 million inhabitants—a gigantic metropolis engulfing the surrounding region. Only one thing is sure: no one can foresee its future.

Zócalo

There's something of the old Tenochtitlán in the heart of the city. The majestic square of the Zócalo is superimposed on the old Aztec marketplace, next to the ruins of the Templo Mayor. Both place of leisure and nerve centre of the city, the Zócalo is graced by some of the most handsome colonial buildings in the whole country.

Every Mexican city has its zócalo; the word comes from the Spanish for plinth or pedestal. Originally, the city planners had decided to set a monument celebrating independence in the middle of the capital's main square. The pedestal was built, but no monument appeared. In vexation, or perhaps in fun, people started to refer to the square as the Zócalo, a name that stuck.

Cathedral

Started in 1573 with materials taken from the Temple of Tláloc-Huitzilopochtli, the cathedral was not completed until two centuries later, which explains the different architectural styles. Three portals pierce the baroque façade built in *tezontle* (a rust-coloured volcanic stone). The adjoining Sagrario is a typical example of the churrigueresque style, a particularly exuberant form of baroque named after the Spanish architect José Churriguera. The nave, more than 100 m (328 ft) long, is flanked by 12 richly ornamented side chapels. Like many other old buildings in the capital, the cathedral is in danger of collapsing: don't be surprised to find it encased in scaffolding and supporting beams.

To the west, a vast colonial building stands on the site of the Axayácatl Palace, where Cortés and his men were lodged in 1519

Construction of the cathedral spanned two and a half centuries, and it incorporates every architectural style from baroque to neoclassical.

and which he adapted and used for his own residence in 1522. Since the 19th century it has housed the Monte de Piedad, the national pawnshop.

National Palace

Stretching along the entire eastern side of the Zócalo, the magnificent National Palace (Palacio Nacional) was the residence of the Spanish viceroys and later of Mexico's presidents. It stands on the site of Montezuma's palace. Built in *tezontle*, it dates from the 16th century but has been remodelled several times. On the staircase and the first floor, 450 sq m (4,830 sq ft) of the walls are covered in murals by Diego Rivera, relating the history of Mexico and daily life in the city before the conquest. The rooms once occupied by Benito Juárez have been transformed into a museum. The palace also houses an art gallery and the National Archives. Outside on the esplanade, usually crawling with street pedlars, shows of Aztec dancing are sometimes organized by associations aiming to preserve pre-Columbian culture.

Templo Mayor

North of the National Palace, a pedestrian street leads to the Templo Mayor, discovered by

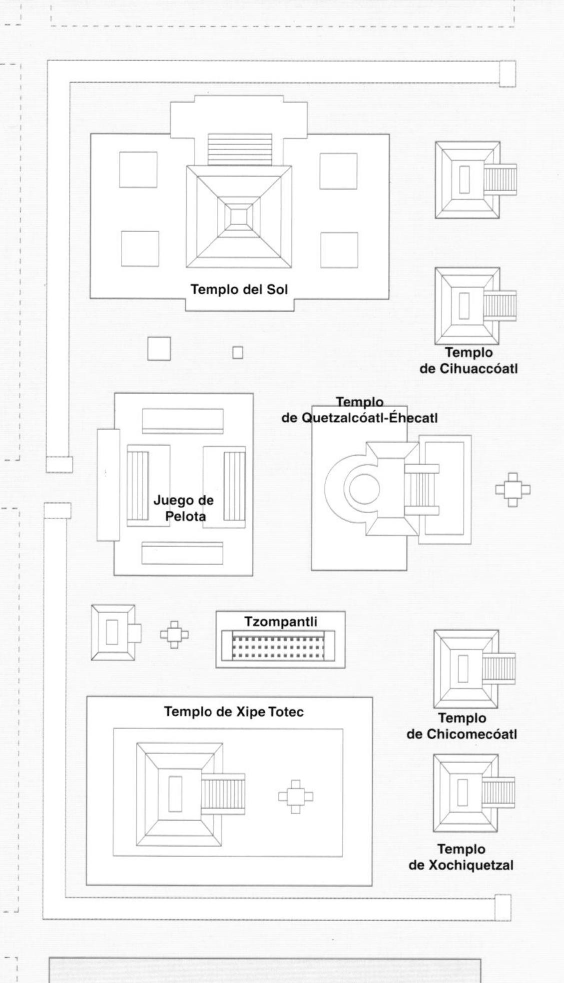
Templo del Sol
Templo
de Cihuaccóatl
Templo
de Quetzalcóatl-Éhecatl
Juego de
Pelota
Tzompantli
Templo de Xipe Totec
Templo
de Chicomecóatl
Templo
de Xochiquetzal
Zócalo

TEMPLO MAYOR

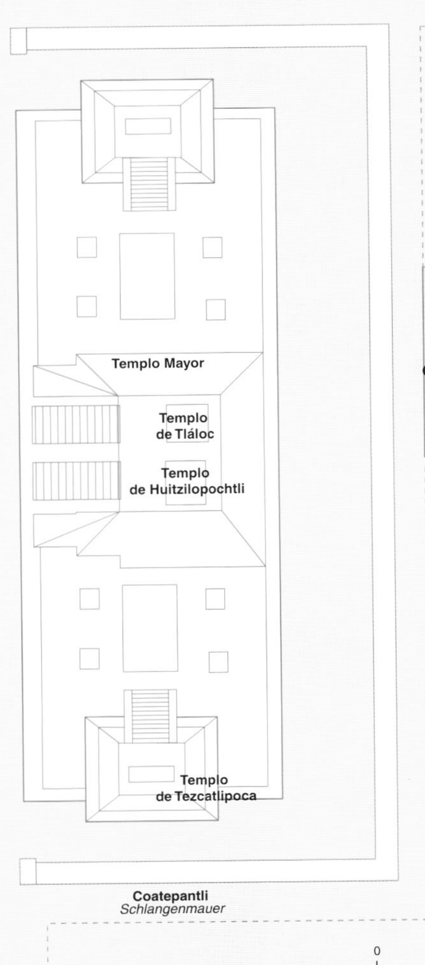

Museo
del Templo Mayor

N

0
100 m

METRO

Mexico's underground public transport system has 104 km (64 miles) of track. You might be surprised by the pictorial signs that are used in the stations. They are designed to help the thousands of newcomers, often illiterate, to find their way around, and are of Aztec inspiration. Another peculiarity of Mexico's Metro: with 4 million passengers a day, things can get rather hairy at rush hour, and some stations reserve special corridors for women and children to prevent their being trampled.

chance in 1978. Workers laying an underground cable unearthed an enormous sculpted stone disc measuring 3.20 m (10.5 ft) in diameter and weighing 8 tonnes, representing the dismembered body of the goddess Coyolxauhqui. Buildings were razed and large-scale excavation was undertaken, bringing to light the most important temple of ancient Tenochtitlán. The Great Temple (Uey Teocalli) was the religious and political centre of the Aztec capital. It is believed to have measured nearly 45 m (147 ft) in height. At the top stood two shrines: that of the rain god Tláloc to the left; and that of Huitzilopochtli, god of sun and war, with its sacrificial altar, to the right. The Templo Mayor commanded an entire complex consisting of ball courts *(juego de pelota)* and ossuaries *(tzompantli)*, long walls on which the skulls of sacrificial victims were aligned on poles, covering an area of 16 ha (40 acres). Archaeologists have uncovered more than 7,000 artefacts from all over the Mexica empire, part of the tribute claimed from conquered peoples.

The ruins reveal one of the main features of Meso-American architecture—there is not one façade, but eleven different layers. Between repairs and commemorative works, each ruler embellished and fortified the Teocalli, covering up the work of his predecessors. A series of raised footpaths offers a good view of the rather confusing whole. The oldest of the structures—and the smallest—is the best conserved.

The museum houses the objects recovered during the digs. Designed on the model of the temple itself, it has two sections, one devoted to Tláloc, the other to Huitzilopochtli. You can see a copy of the Coyolxauhqui monolith (the original is in the Museum of Anthropology) and a scale model of the sacred enclosure.

Old City

One of the best-preserved of the old quarters of the city spreads to the east and north of the Zócalo. Calle Moneda is lined with many colonial buildings and palaces of *tezontle* stone. The Archbishop's Palace faces the old Mint building, which now houses the National Museum of Cultures. The Santísima church is a jewel of churriguresque architecture, its façade thickly encrusted in ornamentation. The Alhóndiga district has been largely restored and is still crossed by some of the canals of ancient Tenochtitlán.

Heading northwest, you pass the National Preparatory School, a former 18th-century Jesuit college noteworthy for its magnificent murals, to reach Plaza Santo Domingo, a square of timeless colonial charm. Public scribes set up their desks beneath the arcades of the palaces looking out onto the plaza. At the far end of the square is a baroque church dating from the 18th century, and closer at hand is the old Palace of the Inquisition, now converted into the Museum of Medicine.

Avenida Pino Suárez

South of the Zócalo, Pino Suárez avenue is the old Ixtapalapán thoroughfare which led to the Templo Mayor. At no. 30, in a restored 18th-century palace, is the Museum of Mexico City, with various collections illustrating the history of the capital and the surrounding valley. Further down, the circular altar of Cihuacóatl, discovered during construction work on the Metro underground, can be seen from the street or from the Pino Suárez station.

To the east, the Merced dates from Aztec days. It's one of the largest fruit and vegetable markets in the world, spreading over 60 city blocks.

Alameda

West of the Zócalo, Avenida Madero has several handsome colonial monuments: at no. 17, the Iturbide Palace (1780) has a superb baroque façade and an attractive interior courtyard. Restored by the Central Bank of Mexico, it has become a cultural centre and hosts numerous exhibitions. At no. 4, the House of the Tiles (Casa de los Azulejos, named after its polychrome tiles), of Spanish-Mudejar inspiration, is one of the oldest buildings in Mexico City. Facing it, the churriguresque San Francisco church is incongruously surrounded by modern buildings.

The avenue opens onto Alameda park, created in 1592 and one of the last large patches of greenery in the city centre. Especially lively at weekends, it is a pleasant place to stroll beneath the gaze of late-19th-century statues. There are several museums in the neighbourhood: the Mexican Museum

TORRE CABALLITO

of Art, housed in a vast Italianate marble palace (8, Calle Tacuba); the Franz Meyer Museum, displaying Mexican furniture, silverware and painting (45, Avenida Hidalgo); the Museum of Arts and Crafts (Artes e Industrias Populares) and the Diego Rivera Museum, where you can admire his most famous work, *Dream of a Sunday Afternoon on the Alameda*. Depicting Rivera as a child, hand-in-hand with Death, it was originally commissioned for the dining room of the Prado Hotel. The hotel was destroyed by the 1985 earthquake but the painting survived intact.

At the western end of the park, near the hansome Cortés Hotel (Avenida Hidalgo), the Viceroyal Art Gallery (Pinacoteca Virreinal) of colonial paintings is housed in a former monastery.

The Palace of Fine Arts (Palacio de Bellas Artes), an imposing building of Carrara marble adorned with bronzes, stands at the other end of the Alameda. It was started in 1900 in preparation for the centennial of independence, but it was not completed until 1934. By then the original architect was dead, which goes to explain why the palace has a classical exterior and an Art Deco interior. It houses an art gallery, with murals by Rivera, Siqueiros, Orozco and Tamayo. Don't miss the theatre and its Tiffany stage curtain, a mosaic of thousands of coloured glass beads. Just before performances of the national folk ballet, light is played on the curtain, representing sunrise and sunset on Popocatépetl and Iztaccíhuatl mountains.

Six blocks north of the Alameda, Garibaldi Square is the favourite gathering place of the *mariachis*: every evening, and Saturday in particular, the musicians hire their services to lovers in need of a cheerful serenade. The atmosphere is hilarious when all the groups are singing at once. There's a long row of tiny restaurants next to the square.

For a view of the whole district, take the lift to the 41st floor of the Latinoamericano tower and its panoramic restaurant, or the observation deck on the next level. On a clear day, you can see as far as Popocatépetl.

Paseo de la Reforma

Further to the west, the Paseo sweeps diagonally across the capital. This Mexican version of the boulevard, 20 km (12 miles) long, was ordered by Maximilian to link the city centre with Chapultepec castle, his official residence. One of the most majestic avenues

A bright flash of modern art at the entrance to Torre Caballito on Paseo de la Reforma.

in the world, it is bordered by the business district, the embassies and the high-class restaurants.

Beyond the intersection with Insurgentes, the pace of the Paseo quickens in the Zona Rosa. During the day, jewellers and exclusive stores provide the glamour. By night, the action shifts to the trendy discos where the golden youth of Mexico City gathers. To the southwest, before reaching the Chapultepec park, you can't miss the 45-m (147-ft) monument to Independence, crowned by a statue of Victory, which the Mexicans call El Angel.

Chapultepec Park

Grasshopper Hill (its name in Náhuatl, the Aztec language) is the oldest and largest park in Mexico city, 400 ha (1000 acres). It is said to have been created at the beginning of the 15th century by Nezahualcóyotl, the poet-king of Texcoco. You can go boating, visit the zoo, a botanical garden and the principal museums of the capital, including one of the best museums in the world: the Museum of Anthropology.

National Museum of Anthropology

This is by far the best of all the city's museums, providing an ideal introduction to the history and art of the pre-Columbian civilizations. Designed by Pedro Ramírez Vázquez and inaugurated in 1964, the building is a formidable work of architecture and the perfect setting for the exhibits, displayed in halls surrounding a central patio.

At ground level, 12 halls retrace the evolution of Meso-America, while an orientation hall allows you to visualize the various exhibits in their original settings, with the aid of scale models and a short film.

It is impossible to take in everything on one visit. You'll have to come back several times if you want to investigate the entire 4 km (2½ miles) of corri-

1

THE BEST MUSEUM In a country as rich in history as Mexico, museums can be counted in their hundreds, but the incomparable **National Museum of Anthropology** in Mexico City stands in a class of its own. The building is an outstanding example of contemporary architecture, and the treasures within include the finest examples of pre-Columbian American art displayed in perfect harmony with their setting.

dors. If time is short, try to concentrate on one particular culture. The Mexica hall displays some of the most important pieces, including the 24-tonne Stone of the Fifth Sun (discovered in 1790 beneath the Zócalo). Also known as the "Aztec Calendar", it depicts, in fact, their conception of the universe.

Other monumental sculptures include the goddess Coatlícue, 2.5 m (8 ft) tall, and the cylindrical Stone of Tizoc, which commemorates the inauguration of the Templo Mayor. See, too, the replica of Montezuma's feather headdress (Cortés sent the original to the king of Spain); the vase in the shape of a jaguar, which served to hold the offerings of human hearts; and the model of the Tlatelolco market, the most important in the empire.

The highlight of the Maya hall is undoubtedly the reproduction of the tomb of Kin Pakal, ruler of Palenque, but don't miss the copies of the frescoes at Bonampak and the lifesize replica of the Temple of Hochob.

The upper floor is devoted to ethnology, comparing contemporary ethnic groups of Mexico with the vanished civilizations.

Chapultepec Castle

At the top of a hill, on a wide esplanade, the "castle" looks out over the city. It was built in 1785 and became the residence of Emperor Maximilian in 1863. Today, the rococo building houses the National Museum of History, which encompasses the history of Mexico from its origins up to the Revolution. Maximilian lived with his wife, Carlota, in the part of the castle called the Alcazar.

Further down the hillside, the Museo de la Lucha del Pueblo Mexicano por la Libertad (generally known more familiarly as El Caracol, "the snail", for the spiral shape of the building) is dedicated to Mexico's struggle for independence.

Other Museums

The Rufino Tamayo Museum presents the artist's own collection of modern paintings, bequeathed to the state on his death from pneumonia in 1991. The permanent exhibits include works by Bacon, Dalí, Giacometti, Magritte, Miró and Picasso, among others.

The David Siqueiros Museum (29, Calle Tres Picos) displays paintings, drawings, lithographs, etc. in what was once the muralist's home.

Other Districts

From the centre to the outskirts, the valley of Mexico and its immediate surroundings offer variety and an abundance of treasures for the traveller.

The Alameda Park is a cool and tranquil oasis in the heart of Mexico City.

Plaza de las Tres Culturas

Nowhere else will you find a sharper view of the contrasting cultures that make up Mexico: this square a few kilometres north of the Zócalo blends Aztec ruins, colonial cathedrals and modern architecture. Tlatelolco, Tenochtitlán's sister city, was the trade centre of the Mexica empire. It was in its marketplace that the final battle against the Spaniards took place.

On the ruins of the city, the conquerors built the Convent of the Holy Cross, a college reserved for the children of the Aztec aristocracy. It is still standing. The church of Santiago Tlatelolco was built in 1609. For a general view of the archaeological site, head for the terrace of the Ministry of Foreign Affairs, from which you can spot the ruins of more temples—one of which, circular in shape, has been restored —and a *tzompantli* where the skulls of sacrificial victims were displayed.

Guadalupe Basilica

On the Tepeyac hill stood an Aztec temple dedicated to Tonantzín. Shortly after the Spanish conquest, the Virgin Mary is said to have appeared here to an Indian, Juan Diego. At first, the bishop of Mexico refused to believe the story, then the Virgin re-appeared and, to convince the disbelievers, she instructed the Indian to gather the roses which had miraculously sprouted up on the spot. When Juan Diego unfolded the cloth in which he had wrapped the flowers, it was imprinted with the image of the Virgin. But it was a dark-skinned Virgin, one with whom the Indians could identify. Since that day, the Virgin of Guadalupe has been the patron saint of Mexico, and Tepeyac has become the venue for the biggest pilgrimage in the country.

The colonial basilica, constructed in *tezontle* stone, dates from 1695. On the verge of crumbling down, it was restored and converted into a museum. The miraculous image was moved to a new basilica, an immense construction which can hold up to 20,000 faithful. To ensure smooth traffic, pilgrims are conveyed on a moving walkway which carries them effortlessly past the image of the Virgin.

Tenayuca Pyramid

Encircled by an impressive band of carved stone serpents, this pyramid was dedicated to the solar cult. It was founded at the beginning of the 12th century by the Chichimecs. Tenayuca served as an architectural model for the Aztecs, and for their Templo Mayor in particular.

The Pyramid of Santa Cecilia Acatitlán, 3 km (2 miles) to the north, is relatively small but features the only Aztec temple that remains intact.

Siqueiros Polyforum

To the south of the city, along Avenida Insurgentes, the Polyforum is part of a vast complex of a somewhat disconcerting modernity. The cultural centre is a 12-sided building, its exterior walls decorated with murals. They all dwell on the theme of mankind's progress, a subject chosen by David Siqueiros for his monumental work on the first floor, which took six years to complete. Combining painting and relief sculpture, it is commented by a sound and light show while you view it from a moving platform.

Coyoacán

Coyoacán ("the place of the coyotes"), 8 km (5 miles) south of Mexico City, is a picturesque colonial district of streets paved with pebbles and bordered by 17th- and 18th-century houses. The town hall on the central square is said to have been the home of Hernán Cortés. The San Juan Bautista church south of the Zócalo was founded in 1530 by Dominican fathers. On La Conchita square stands the pretty church of La Concepción, with a churriguresque façade.

The Frida Kahlo Museum at 127, Calle Londres displays numerous paintings by the famous painter, wife of Diego Rivera, in addition to the couple's collection of pre-Columbian art and modern painting. Mexican muralists were politically committed, and Rivera was a good friend of Trotsky, who lived in exile in Mexico. He dwelled nearby (at 45, Calle Viena), and it was there he was murdered in 1940. He is buried in the garden. His home was left undisturbed after his death, and is now a museum.

Churubusco

East of Coyoacán, Churubusco has another well-preserved district, especially the area around the Franciscan monastery (partially reconverted into the Museum of Foreign Imperialism).

Anahuacalli Museum

This exceptional museum, 3 km (2 miles) to the south, houses, in a building built of *tezontle* and fashioned after a pyramid, a large collection of pre-Columbian antiques bequeathed by Diego Rivera just before his death.

EARTHQUAKE

At 7.19 a.m. on September 19, 1985, an earthquake registering 8.1 on the Richter scale destroyed entire sectors of the capital in a few seconds.

On the same latitudes as Mexico, the Cocos oceanic plate thrusts beneath the continental plate, causing numerous earth tremors. Moreover, two coastal zones present a troubling geological anomaly: no earth tremors have been felt there in a long time. This is literally the calm before the storm—it means that the Cocos plate has met with an underwater obstacle and that the pressure is building up. The *terremoto* of 1985 struck when the tension caused a similar restraint to snap, so another earthquake of comparable magnitude is obviously imminent.

Mexico is unfortunate in that it is built on a terrain of very soft clay. According to recent studies, it would seem that this factor contributes to increasing the speed and force of seismic movements. The official death toll of the 1985 quake was 4,500, though officiously the figure of 8,000 was mentioned, while some rumours spoke of as many as 40,000 deaths. More than 1,000 buildings collapsed, and 500,000 people were left homeless. The disaster exposed the total disregard for earthquake-proof construction methods as well as widespread corruption: almost all the hospitals were destroyed as well.

San Angel

West of Coyoacán, San Angel is another colonial town submerged by the capital's relentless expansion. It's a residential area, full of well-to-do Chilangos and a great many artists. An arts and crafts market (Bazar Sábado) is held every Saturday on Plaza San Jacinto. On the western side of the square, the church, fringed by a pleasant garden, was part of a convent founded at the end of the 16th century. On the northern side, Casa del Risco, a museum displaying Mexican and European artefacts, has two patios and a splendid porcelain fountain.

Plaza del Carmen is the site of the finest architectural jewel of San Angel: the Carmel Convent, built in 1615 and crowned by three cupolas. It has 17th-century frescoes, attractive cloisters with a tile-covered fountain and, in the crypt, the mummified remains of 18th-century church dignitaries.

To the north, at 1608, Avenida Revolución, the Carrillo Gil Museum has a good collection of 20th-century artists—Kandinsky, Rodin and Picasso, among others.

To the west of the centre, the Estudio Diego Rivera Museum has been set up in the painter's studio. Nearby, the San Angel Inn is a classy restaurant in a superb 18th-century baroque *hacienda*. At 18 Calle Lazcano, the Casa de los Delfines (House of the Dolphins) is an attractive mansion of the same period, with a tropical park.

On an old lava field *(pedregal)* south of San Angel, now covered with gardens, are some of the most sumptuous villas of the country. One of the earliest settlements in the Mexico Basin (from around 1200 BC) was discovered near here, at Copilco.

University

To the west of the lava field, the University Campus of Mexico City covers 300 ha (740 acres) and educates nearly 350,000 students! Built in the early 1950s, the 80 buildings housing the various departments symbolize the ideal of social justice in countless positivist and patriotic frescoes. Especially worth seeing is the three-dimensional painting by David Siquieros in the Rectorate, and the mosaic on the prism-shaped Library, illustrating the history of Mexico. The campus is also the site of the 80,000-seat Olympic Stadium.

Cuicuilco Pyramid

Cuicuilco was probably one of the principal cities in the Mexico Valley from 600 to 100 BC, when it was buried by lava after a volcanic eruption. A conical pyramid, 23m (75 ft) high, has been excavated, and a small museum displays the finds.

CENTRAL PLATEAU

Teotihuacán and the North, Puebla and the East, Xochimilco and the South, Taxco and the West

Many of Mexico's most interesting sites are within a radius of about 100 km (60 miles) of Mexico City. Teotihuacán—the cradle of the Meso-American civilization must not be missed, but its successors are also well worth a detour: Cholula and its great pyramid, Xochicalco, Teotenango, Tula, Malinalco, and so on.

As a counterpoint to the pre-Columbian cities, this region harbours some of the most loveliest towns built by the Spaniards during their colonial era—Puebla, an architectural pearl; Tlaxcala; Cuernavaca and the silver city of Taxco. The missionary zeal of the conquerors later dispersed to the mountain slopes, inspiring the convents and monasteries of Acolman, Actopan, Tepotzotlán, and so on.

This section makes a clockwise tour of the best sights in the high plateau around the capital, starting in the north.

Teotihuacán and the North

The largest pre-Columbian city in the country, 50 km (30 miles) northeast of Mexico City, remains something of an enigma as regards its builders and their culture. Recent studies suggest that its development began in the 1st century BC, reaching its greatest period of glory in the 6th century AD. It then underwent a sudden decline, which still goes unexplained. The Aztecs rediscovered the city later and, awed by its enormous dimensions, they named it Teotihuacán ("the place where the gods were created").

Pyramid of the Sun

Teotihuacán was designed according to a careful plan: all its monuments are oriented following a cosmogonical pattern centred around the Pyramid of the Sun, the oldest structure, some 65 m (213 ft) high. It stands on a raised platform measuring 350 m (1,150 ft) each side, and the west façade is sited directly opposite the point on the horizon where the sun sets when it passes its zenith.

A mysterious underground passage, discovered only in 1971, leads from the base of the main stairway to a cave in the shape of a four-leaf clover (not open to visitors) under the very centre of the pyramid. Archaeologists believe this natural cavern-turned-shrine was the sanctum sanctorum of the Teotihuacanos—the place where the world was born.

The Pyramids of the Sun and the Moon at Teotihuacán, the "City of the Gods".

Way of the Dead

The magnificent view from the top of the temple takes in the main thoroughfare of the city: the Way of the Dead (Miccaótli), bordered by the remains of stone buildings. It was thus named by the Aztecs who believed that the buildings were tombs, but in fact the structures are the foundations of ancient temples. The avenue, 45–55 m (147–180 ft) wide, runs nearly 2 km (over a mile) from the Pyramid of the Moon in the north, to the Citadel at the southern extreme of the city.

Probably to comply with some astrological requirement, the course of the San Juan river which runs through the site was diverted so that it intersected the avenue at right angles.

Ceremonial Centre

At 45 m (147 ft), the Pyramid of the Moon is smaller than the Pyramid of the Sun, but their tops are at the same level due to the natural incline of the Way of the Dead. It was built somewhat later (around the year 300). To the west of the plaza, the Palace of Quetzalpapálotl (Feathered Butterfly) probably served as a residence for the high priests. Note the carvings of the butterfly deity. Just behind this palace are the Palace of the Jaguars and the

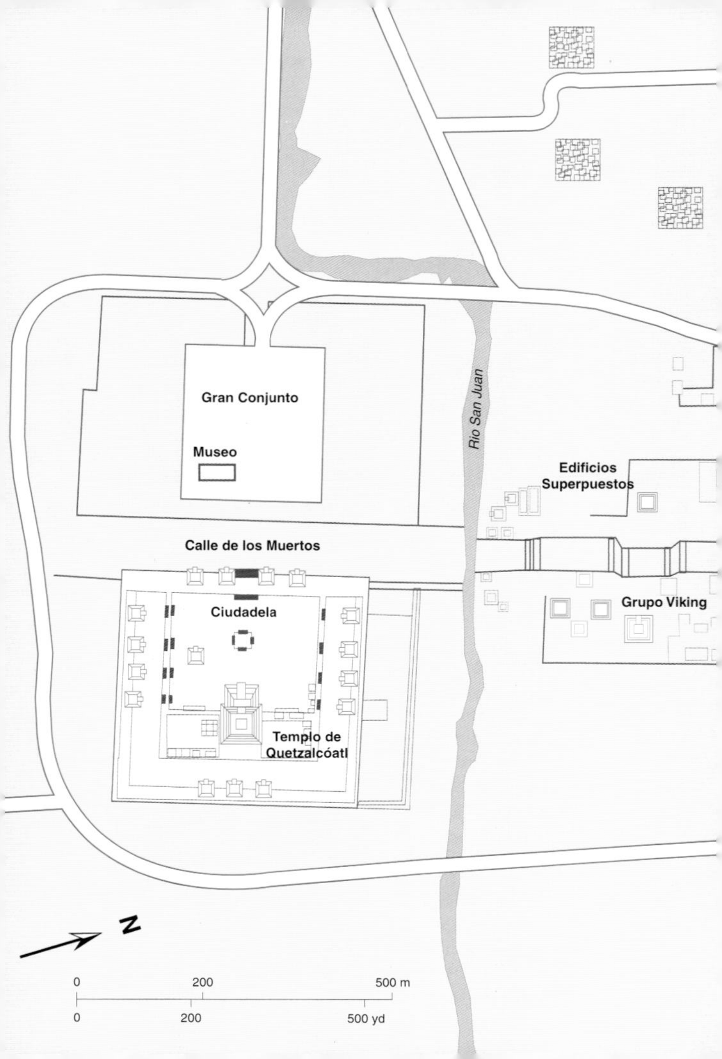
Gran Conjunto
Museo
Río San Juan
Edificios
Superpuestos
Calle de los Muertos
Ciudadela
Grupo Viking
Templo de
Quetzalcóatl
N
0
200
500 m
0
200
500 yd

TEOTIHUACÁN

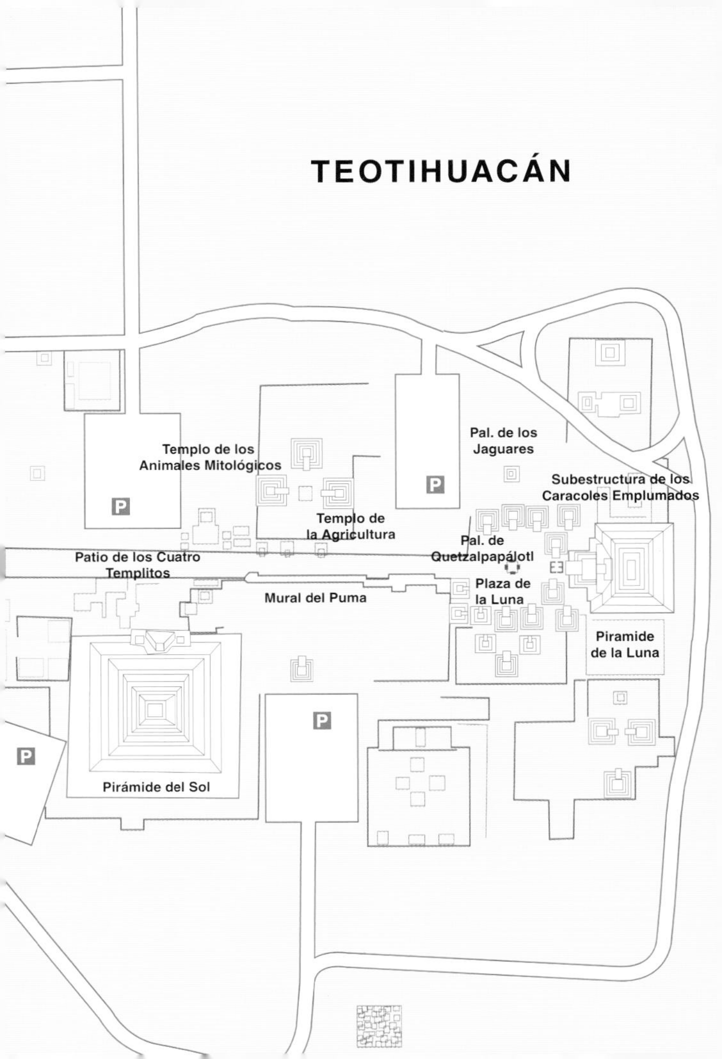

Temple of the Feathered Shells (Caracoles Emplumados), with remains of mural paintings.

To the south of the Miccaótli, the Citadel was part of an immense complex completed in the year 250. Named by the conquistadors, who mistook its four platforms for fortifications, the structure in fact incorporated a forum, administrative buildings and the Temple of Quetzalcóatl, almost entirely covered by a later pyramid (complying with the tenets of pre-Columbian building methods). On four levels of the pyramid, archaeologists have uncovered remarkable carvings of feathered serpents. There are also some traces of painting which give a hint of the original polychrome colouring of the reliefs and carvings.

Facing the citadel, on the site of the old market place, is the museum, with a model of the site, plus copies of statues and numerous ritual artefacts.

QUETZALCÓATL

The best known of the Mexican gods combines myth and history. The Feathered Serpent (a name derived from *quetzal*, symbol of the sun) is the Creator, and he also taught men science, morality, and the cultivation of corn. Yet, varying with the period or local custom, he also became identified with the god of the wind, movement, the dawn, spring and rebirth. The great civilizer, he embodied human ideals and man's spirituality. According to legend, he was forced to flee Tula, leaving his kingdom at the mercy of his enemy Tezcatlipoca, who had an insatiable appetite for human sacrifices. Quetzalcóatl set off over the Celestial Waters, only to return to reclaim his kingdom—in the unlikely form of Hernán Cortés.

Surroundings

Outside the ceremonial centre, Teotihuacán was divided into working and residential districts, in turn subdivided into different districts and dwellings. Each district was devoted to a particular activity: Tetitla to the brewing of *pulque*, an alcoholic beverage made from the agave; Atetelco to obsidian carving, and so forth. Numerous remains of paintings represent men, animals, nature and gods. In the Museum of Anthropology in Mexico City, there is a copy of the most famous, the *Paradise of Tláloc*.

Acolman

On the road to Mexico City, some 10 km (6 miles) from Teotihuacán, the Monastery of Acolman was one of the first founded by the Augustinians in Mexico, in 1539. Its imposing church has a beautiful, though rather sober, Renaissance façade. There are 16th-century frescoes at the back of the nave and in the cloisters.

Tepotzotlán

North of Mexico City, Tepotzotlán is an old colonial town that has now been absorbed into the capital's suburbs. Even so, it has managed to retain its charm and possesses, in the San Francisco Javier church, one of the country's most outstanding examples of churriguresque architecture. Covered in a veritable explosion of carvings, it was built at the end of the 17th century and remodelled in the baroque style a hundred years later. Inside, the gilded altarpieces and the painted ceilings are the epitome of this extravagant style.

The adjacent monastery and its chapel have been converted into the Viceroyal Museum of Colonial Painting.

Tula

The experts don't seem to agree on the origins of the Toltec capital, but it appears to have been founded around the year 900 by a tribe which had come from the north. Topiltzín, the most famous of its rulers, worshipped Quetzalcóatl, to the point where he is sometimes confused with the god himself. Forced from his kingdom by the priests of the bloodthirsty Tezcatlipoca ("Smoking Mirror", the god of war), the king swore that one day he would return. This gave rise to the legend that would later transform Hernan Cortés into a divine envoy in the eyes of the Aztecs. At some undetermined date, the theocratic Toltec state developed into a warrior nation, and probably introduced wholesale human sacrifices. Tula was destroyed around 1168 during a Chichimec invasion.

The ruins, relatively small, are located on the top of a hill overlooking the surrounding valley

THE TWO MOST BEAUTIFUL PYRAMIDS

Pyramids come in all sizes in Mexico, and many of them are exceptional. But from the top of the **Pyramid of the Moon** in Teotihuacán, you see the splendour of the ancient city, spreading out in front of the **Pyramid of the Sun**. In the quiet of the early morning you can imagine what life was like here 2,000 years ago, when the pyramids were covered in coloured stucco.

landscape. Grouped around a large square are a ball court, the burnt palace (notice the two *chacmools*, reclining figures which served as sacrificial altars), and the Temple of Tlahuizcalpantecuhtli, perched at the top of a small, five-tiered pyramid. On the upper platform are four *atlantes*, carved columns, which originally supported the roof of the temple. They portray Quetzalcóatl in his manifestation as the morning star. To the north, the 40-m (130-ft) Coatepantli—Wall of Serpents—is adorned with geometric patterns and carved snakes devouring human skeletons. To the south are the sparse remains of the Templo Mayor. The small on-site museum (to the left of the entrance) has displays of Toltec and Aztec sculptures and ceramics.

Actopan

North of the Mexico Basin, the large Otomí town of Actopan boasts a striking 16th-century fortified monastery. The church has an attractive plateresque façade and the cloister conserves some of the most beautiful frescoes of this period in Mexico (also in the open chapel). There is a museum of Otomí arts and crafts as well.

Further north, Ixmilquilpan has a similar, if smaller monastery. The Monday market is a lively meeting place for all the Indians of the area.

IXTLE

The all-purpose agave plant provides, among othe things, the *ixtle* fibres with which the Indians traditionally made fabrics. Even today, in the mountains of the Mexquital valley, Otomí women weave the fibres to make garments called *ayate* or brightly coloured belts. Embroidery is done with a needle made from a cactus thorn.

Puebla and the East

Founded in the first years of the conquest (1531), Puebla is one of the Mexican cities most marked by its Spanish heritage. A major Catholic centre, developed as the counterpoint of the pre-Spanish town of Cholula. The dozens of clocktowers, cupolas, cathedrals and homes of the old Creole aristocracy are ornamented with *azulejo* tiles in a style that is typical of the city.

City Centre

Start your visit in the Zócalo, one of the most outstanding in the country, surrounded by 16th-century arcades. The Renaissance cathedral, with later baroque touches, was started around 1580 and completed in 1649. Across the street, at no. 2, the Casa del que mató el animal (House of the one who killed the animal) has a

Renaissance portal with sides and lintel carved with hunting scenes that look as though they were inspired by a 15th-century French tapestry. South of the cathedral, the former Archbishop's Palace now houses the superb Palafox Library, created in 1646, with exhibits of works dating back to the beginnings of the printing press. The nearby Amparo Museum is devoted to the history of Mexico.

East of the Zócalo, the Casa de los Muñecos (House of Dolls) has a magnificent fresco in *azulejo* tiles. Walking down Avenida Camacho, you reach the Compañía church, noteworthy for its churriguresque façade and its dome covered in white and blue tiles. The adjoining University dates from the 16th century (note the wide patio).

To the northeast, the Casa del Afeñique is a remarkable example of *poblana* architecture, with its typical coloured tile façade. Nearby are the theatre (1756) and the plateresque San Francisco church.

Two blocks north of the Zócalo, adjoining the baroque Church of Santo Domingo, the Rosario chapel, built at the end of the 17th century, is undoubtedly the most spectacular building in Puebla. The interior, groaning under the weight of a profusion of gold, is enlivened by heavenly hosts of sculpted cherubs and angels.

Past the covered market of Victoria, the Santa Rosa convent is famous throughout the country as the place where the nuns reinvented *mole poblano*, a savoury sauce based on a pre-Spanish recipe which incorporates chocolate and spices. The pretty 17th-century building has been converted into a museum of folk art. Every possible surface is adorned with tiles in the courtyard and the extraordinary kitchen.

The Santa Monica convent, consecrated in 1609—and now a museum—also has a handsome patio with walls covered in *azulejo* tiles.

Guadalupe Hill

Overlooking Puebla in the northeast, the forts of Loreto and Guadalupe were the scene of one of the rare military victories in Mexican history: on May 5, 1862 the Juarista army crushed the French expeditionary force sent by Napoleon III. Later, the fort of Loreto was converted into a museum of history, and May 5 became the Mexican national holiday. The Museum of the State of Puebla houses interesting collections of local antiquities.

Cholula

Cholula, 10 km (6 miles) west of Puebla, was one of the principal pre-Columbian religious centres of the central plateau, reaching its peak around the year 600. At the time of the conquest, the city still had nearly 100,000 inhabitants and, according to Cortés, 400 pyramids. Cholula was destroyed by the conquistadors, never to rise again.

The city is the site of the most impressive pyramid in Mexico, 60 m (196 ft) high, but mainly buried under a hill. You can only see the excavated base. The old temple on top of the pyramid was razed and replaced with the shrine of Los Remedios.

In the Cholula region, many villages have attractive examples of *poblana* architecture. Visit the churches of Tlaxcalancingo (18th century); San Francisco Acatepec, richly ornamented in brick and tile; and above all Santa María Tonantzintla, with its profusion of decorative motifs, scrolls and arabesques intertwined with colourful cherubs, the work of many generations of Indian artists.

Huejotzingo

On the road to Mexico City, Huejotzingo is the site of one of the country's most attractive 16th-century Franciscan monasteries. In plateresque style, the building shows traces of mural paintings. Its fortified church has superb Gothic vaults, and the atrium adjoins the four *posas* (oratories), of Moorish inspiration.

Tlaxcala

The ancient Tlaxcalec Confederation, an enclave in Aztec territory, used to fight periodical ritual combats with Montezuma's soldiers. The aim of these so-called "Flower Wars" was to provide the gods' altars with a fresh supply of sacrificial victims. Tlaxcala allied itself with the conquistadors and rapidly developed after the Aztecs' downfall. As a consequence, every trace of the city's pre-Hispanic past has disappeared. It is, however, rich in colonial history. The charming Zócalo, the San Francisco convent—one of the oldest in the country—and San José church are all interesting to visit.

In Ocotlán, near Tlaxcala, stands an 18th-century church which is the venue for a major annual pilgrimage. It has a magnificent churriguresque façade. The only pre-Columbian relics to be found in the area are at Tizatlán, 4 km (2½ miles away), where the palace of the governor Xicoténcatl and several murals remain.

Cacaxtla

Capital of a nation of Maya extraction from 650 to 850, Cacaxtla is mainly known for its well-preserved frescoes. The paintings portray individual personages as well as battle scenes, whose colours are surprisingly vivid.

Popocatépetl

On a clear day, the view of the most distinguished of Mexican volcanoes is incomparable. Towering over the plateau at 5,452 m (17,886 ft), it can be seen for many miles around. Its twin, Iztaccíhuatl, reaches an equally dizzy 5,286 m (17,342 ft).

A legend recounts the story of Iztaccíhuatl, the daughter of an emperor, who died of a broken heart when she was led to believe she would never again set eyes upon Popocatépetl, a warrior with whom she was in love. Upon his safe return, he undertook the construction of two mountains: one to serve as the tomb of the young princess, and the other for himself, bearing the eternal flame of his grief (you may still see a plume of smoke today).

Before laying siege to Tenochtitlán, Cortés sent two men tied to a rope down into the crater of Popocatépetl—which was in eruption at the time—to gather sulphur to make gunpowder for his cannons. The volcano was inactive for many years, but woke from its slumber in 1997, and so hikers can no longer get close to the cone.

Xochimilco and the South

Xochimilco, 30 km (20 miles) south of Mexico City, is renowned for its floating gardens, a reminder of the pre-Columbian Venice that was Tenochtitlán. Artificial rafts of mud and reeds, the *chinampas* were first planted with flowers and vegetables in the 8th century by a people related to the Aztecs. The roots grew down to the bottom of the freshwater lagoon, anchoring them permanently. Today, less than a thousand *chinampas* are still cultivated (originally there were 15,000). Families come from the capital for barge-trips in this marshy setting. The canals are especially lively at weekends, when assiduous mariachis and persuasive pedlars hitch themselves to your barge.

Back on dry land, do not miss the colourful Saturday market.

Cuernavaca

The capital of the state of Morelos, Cuernavaca has always been a popular resort for rest and relaxation. Aztec princes came here to benefit from its waters. Cortés had a residence built here, and Maximilian came for the summer. The "City of Eternal Spring", as Alexander von Humboldt described it, is still one of the favourite retreats of well-to-do Chilangos. Its charm has faded somewhat with the arrival of industry, but there is still good sightseeing in the city centre.

On the eastern side of the Zócalo, the Palace of Cortés is a big medieval-style fortress which be-

BIENVENIDOS
LUCERITO

longed to the conquistador himself and later to his estate up to the end of the 19th century. Since then it has housed the Cuauhnáhuac Museum, with archaeological collections as well as exhibitions illustrating the more recent past. Upstairs, a superb fresco by Diego Rivera takes up the historical theme. The cathedral, started in 1530 and one of the oldest in Mexico, was a centre of intense missionary activity. Next to it, the Borda Garden was laid out towards the end of the 18th century by the son of a silver magnate. The estate, which was Maximilian's summer residence, is typical of the Creole aristocracy.

The Pyramid of Teopanzolco, east of the city centre, dates from the Aztec period. Like many others, it consists of two superimposed pyramids. Southwest of the city centre, you can visit a museum devoted to herbal lore, in a small country house built by Maximilian for clandestine meetings with his Indian mistress.

Tepoztlán

A Tlahuica mountain village, Tepoztlán was an ancient place of pilgrimage for the Aztecs, who came here to venerate Tepozteco, god of agriculture and *pulque*. If you have a few hours to spare, take the steep road to the top of Cerro del Tepozteco at 2,100 m (6,890 ft), where you find the ruins of the god's shrine, a small pyramid. A spectacular fiesta is held here every year to celebrate the end of the harvest (the night of 7–8 September).

In town, visit the formidable Dominican convent, today a museum of pre-Columbian culture.

Xochicalco

In a wild and rugged setting, the "Place of the House of Flowers" (its name in Náhuatl) is historically one of the most important of the central plateau. From the fall of Teotihuacán to the emergence of the Toltec nation, it formed a link between these two civilizations, a great crossroads for culture, trade and religion. It's believed that dignitaries representing the Zapotec, Maya and peoples of the Tierras Calientes met here around 650 to synchronize their respective calendars.

Dominating the main square, the Pyramid of the Feathered Serpent is the most interesting monument. Note the superb carvings, which were originally painted. A number of underground passages lead to chambers whose purpose is uncertain (perhaps to observe the equinoxes). South of the plaza is a large ball court.

The "floating village" of Xochimilco is all that remains of the Aztec city of Tenochtitlán.

Taxco and the West

Perched on a series of hills, the town of Taxco was for many years the silver capital of Mexico. Miners were sent here by Cortés to search for tin to make cannons, but instead they stumbled on one of the richest silver deposits in all of New Spain. Quickly, their camp grew into a proper village, then a city. The vein became exhausted and it wasn't until the 18th century that a second silver-rush overwhelmed Taxco. Enter José de la Borda, an adventurer who had left France aged 16. He accumulated a great fortune, spending much of it on beautifying Taxco. (It was his son that designed the Borda Garden in Cuernavaca). Then, once more, this city of steep and narrow streets slipped back into oblivion. It has been resuscitated as a handicrafts centre, where silver items are produced in 300 workshops.

Charming, picturesque, extravagant—Taxco is all these and more. It is a gem of colonial art. A labyrinth of cobblestone alleys clings to the hillside, and round every corner, plunging views are revealed over an expanse of red-tiled rooftops, interrupted by the domes of churches. Taxco has been declared a national monument. But nothing can rival the vista from Monte Taxco, reached by cable car. On a clear day, you can see as far as Popocatépetl.

Centre

On one side of the Zócalo (Plaza de la Borda), the church of Santa Prisca is a churriguresque masterpiece. It was built in the 1750s by José de la Borda, and no expense was spared. The rosy façade is a riot of baroque ornamentation and the towers are a veritable lacework in stone. Inside, nine glittering altarpieces are stuccoed with scrolls, volutes, fruit, shells, leaves, vines and cherubs.

Graceful colonial homes, including Don José's, line the other sides of the Zócalo. The Museo Guillermo Spratling contains displays of pre-Columbian art and historical displays. Spratling, an American, set up a silver workshop and taught the local craftsmen to incorporate ancient designs into their products. The small Museum of Silver dwells on the tribulations of the country's mining history.

You'll find jeweller's shops *(platerías)* in every street, especially around the Craftsmen's Patio. Near Plaza de los Gallos, the Casa de Figueroa (1767) was once the mint. Explore at your leisure this district where you'll discover several buildings full of character and charm.

Caves

At Cacahuamilpa, 30 km (20 miles) from Taxco, a vast network of caves stretches underground. Take a guided tour to explore the immense halls with fascinating coloured rock formations, stalactites and stalagmites.

Malinalco

Perched on a steep peak in a desolate valley, the ruins of Malinalco's ceremonial centre count among the most interesting Aztec sites. The main temple, carved out of the rock, was dedicated to the military and religious orders of the Eagles and the Jaguars. New recruits, the sons of noble families, were initiated here. You reach the underground hall through the carved, open mouth of a serpent with menacing fangs, its tongue trailing along the floor. You can see also the Tzinacalli, sanctuary of the knights of the order, and the Temple of the Sun.

Teotenango

The ancient Matlazinca principality, overlooking the Valley of Toluca, had its heyday at the close of the first millennium, falling later into Aztec hands. The remains of the city, successfully restored, are impressive: wide squares, tiered pyramids, a ball court and even a steam bath which served a religious as well as medicinal purpose.

Toluca

At an altitude of over 2600 m (8,530 ft), this city some 60 km (40 miles) west of the capital has a pleasant centre within industrial surroundings. An early-1900s iron market hall with stained-glass windows has been reconverted into a charming botanical garden. Toluca is best known for its Indian market (daily, although most effervescent on Friday), humming with activity in the early hours of the morning. Handicrafts are well represented.

Calixtlahuaca

The remains of this hybrid city, made up of an old Matlazinca district and an Aztec garrison, have an amazing round sanctuary referred to as the Temple of Quetzalcóatl, the ruins of the Temple of Tláloc and a beautiful Mexica *tzompantli*.

Nevado de Toluca

A mountain road takes you through a pleasant landscape to the top of this inactive volcano, at 4,260 m (1,400 ft). In the bowl of the crater there are two pretty lakes. From the top, the view seems to reach forever.

Desierto de los Leones

Heading back towards Mexico City, a pleasant stop in the pine forest of this national park gives you, apart from wonderful views, the chance to explore the Convent of Nuestra Señora del Carmen, built in the 17th century.

ACAPULCO
Plaza Pie
de la Cuesta
Zihuatanejo
Avenida Ejido
Av. Constituyentes
Calzada Pie de la Cuesta
Av. Cuauhtémoc
Parque Papagayo
Av. Cuauhtémoc
Paseo del Farallón
México
EL VELADERO
Centro Acapulco
Campo de Golf
Oficina de Tourismo
Costera Miguel Alemán
Av. Costera Miguel Alemán
Hornos
La Condesa
Morro Chico
Farallón de San Lorenzo
Centro Cultural y de Convenciones
La Redonda
Farallón del Obispo
Museo Arqueológico
CICI
Parque La Iguana
Fuerte de San Diego
Mateos Quebrada
Mercado de Curiosidades
Catedral
ZÓCALO
Puerto
Icacos
La Quebrada
Bahía de Acapulco
El Chivato
La Caba
Costera Miguel Alemán
Honda
Aguada
Piedra del Elefante
Avenida López
Punta Grifo
Punta del Guitarrón
Playuelita
Arena Coliso
Plaza de Toros Caletilla
Av. Adolfo López Mateos
La Poma
Carretera Escénica
Caleta
Caletilla
Virgén Submarina
N
Canal de Boca Chica
Isla Verbabuena
La Roqueta
Puerto Marqués,
Acapulco Princess Hotel,
Playa Revolcadero
0
2 km
Isla de La Roqueta

THE PACIFIC COAST

Acapulco, Southeast Coast, Northwest Coast

From Huatulco in the south to Mazatlán in the north, the Pacific Ocean bathes more than 1500 km (930 miles) of a shoreline that seems to have been invented for leisure and holidaymaking. Starting with the famous resort city of Acapulco, this section sets out to discover the Oaxaca coast, travelling up the coast to stop at beach resorts and fishing villages.

Acapulco

The setting of Mexico's best-known resort is famous around the world: a perfect sheltered bay of golden beaches and swaying palm trees, against a background of mountains and of deep blue sea, flanked by rocky ramparts plunging into the sea.

Peninsula de las Playas

To the west, the peninsula juts out into the ocean as if to protect the old town. A veritable shield of cliffs, it has magnificent sandy coves, perfectly safe for swimmers. It was here that the city's first hotels were built during the 1950s, and the place retains the atmosphere of a seaside resort on a human scale. One of the principal attractions—apart from the beach, of course—is to watch the ritual of the *clavadistos*, death-defying divers, who throw themselves off the 35-m (114-ft) cliff of La Quebrada. They perform at fixed hours: at 1 p.m. and at one-hour intervals in the evening from 7.30 to 10.30 p.m.

During the day, you can enjoy your favourite sports. Playa Caleta, one of the most popular beaches, has every option imaginable: water-skiing, jet-skiing, diving, canoeing off the island of La Roqueta, or sailing. You can also take a trip in a glass-bottomed boat to view the submerged statue of the Virgin of Guadalupe.

To the west, the coastal route leads to Pie de la Cuesta, on a tongue of land enclosing the Coyuca lagoon. The beach stretches into the distance in an idyllic setting, and a boat trip on the lagoon's tranquil waters reveals a wealth of birdlife. Watching the sunset here has become something of a tradition. But be careful: it's dangerous to go swimming.

Zócalo

In the centre of Acapulco, the old Fort of San Diego (1616), all that remains of the city's rich past, recalls that this was where the *naos*, or galleons, from the Philippines, Peru and Chile put into port. Their cargoes of gold, silver, silk

The Bay of Acapulco curves in a graceful crescent.

and porcelain brought prosperity to the city but also attracted the unwelcome attention of pirates, despite the fortress built to defend it. The Museum of History is devoted to the story of the city's trade with the Orient. It also recalls the earthquake of 1776, and the bewildering times when the port's ties with the Spanish world were cut following Mexico's independence.

From the seafront promenade, the Malecón, numerous operators organise mini-cruises around the bay, as well as deep sea fishing trips. Back from the seafront there is a charming crafts market, the Mercado de Curiosidades.

The Bay

All along the sandy stretch to the east, an extravagant succession of luxury hotels, swimming pools and tropical gardens spaces out over some 15 km (10 miles). Here you will find the most popular beaches—Hornos, Hornitos, La Condesa, Icacos—where all sorts of leisure and sports activities are available.

You can also stroll in the Papagayo Park (botanical garden, lake, cable car, children's rides, etc.) or take your kids to the CICI, a large marine amusement park. Archaeology buffs can visit the Cultural Centre, featuring a collection of pre-Columbian art and a hall with temporary exhibitions. The Convention Hall (Centro Internacional) houses a crafts gallery, various exhibition halls and a theatre.

Beyond the promontory closing the eastern end of the bay, Puerto Marqués beach is pleasant for swimming (if you swim elsewhere, watch out for the undertow). On the way there, the panoramic route affords unequalled views over Acapulco. Further still, the Playa Revolcadero beach stretches on infintely.

Southeast Coast

The Oaxaca coast has been slowly awakening to tourism for the past two decades, with development most advanced and luxurious at Huatulco.

Puerto Escondido

This former fishing village nestling at the heart of a pretty bay surrounded by hills is gradually becoming into a popular holiday destination. Fortunately for the little port, the tropical setting and crystal-clear waters have so far resisted change.

Puerto Angelito beach, to the west, is the safest for swimming. In the other direction, Zicatela beach is preferred by surfers, but there's a dangerous undertow. In general, it isn't advised to go for a solitary walk along the beach, especially in the evening.

Puerto Angel

Some 70 km (43 miles) to the east, Puerto Angel is a small port in a charming setting. Two rocky capes guard the entrance to its bay lined with a fine sand beach against a background of lush vegetation. Tourism is still in its infancy here, and the facilities are fairly basic, which, for many, adds to the place's attractions. The main activity is simply lazing on the numerous beaches, of which Zipolite, fringed by palm trees, is the best known. But don't swim in these treacherous waters.

Huatulco

A string of eight splendid bays is witnessing the birth of a new super-resort in the style of Cancún. Luxury homes are sprouting beside the exceptionally beautiful—and tranquil—beaches without infringing on the harmony of the surroundings. An airport has been built, and a golf course opened. For the moment, development is centred around Santa Cruz Huatulco, the only bay with a port. Tangolunga Bay has several exclusive hotels.

Northwest Coast

Northwest of Acapulco along a coastal route bordered by coconut palms, the sites of Ixtapa and Zihuatenejo, fairly close together, offer an entirely different aspect of the Pacific coast.

MEXCALTITAN

A little island on a lagoon, surrounded by tropical forest, Mexcaltitán, "the land of the moon", is, according to some legends, the original homeland of the Aztecs. Nicknamed the Venice of Mexico —because, in the rainy season, its streets turn into canals —the village matches the old descriptions of the mythical Aztlán, the Place of the Herons, from which was derived the name Aztec.

Zihuatanejo

The convivial atmosphere of Zihuatanejo's past as a small port has been preserved. Tucked away in the depths of a pretty, sheltered bay, the resort has a handful of white sand beaches, of which La Ropa and Las Gatas are the best for swimming. Don a mask and flippers for a memorable diving experience: at the confluence of several currents, the marine life here is varied and the visibility excellent. Zihuatanejo is also a well-known base for deep-sea fishing trips.

Ixtapa

Like Huatulco, Ixtapa is one of success stories of the Mexican Ministry of Tourism. Opulent hotels are strung along the 6-km (4-mile) Playa del Palmar. The golf course and marina are tastefully laid out. To the west, the sandy beaches of Don Juan, Casa Blanca and Cuata snuggle in sheltered coves. Offshore, Ixtapa Island is a favourite destination for sun worshippers.

Manzanillo

A large commercial port wedged between a lagoon and the ocean, Manzanillo has also started promoting itself as a beach resort. Its facilities are rather limited for the moment; they are grouped around Santiago Bay and on the fringes of Playa Azul. The city is known for deep-sea fishing: there's a big swordfishing competition every November.

To the north, Barra de Navidad and Melaque are two other small family resorts where sunbathing and lazing around are the main activities if you are not tempted by surfing or fishing.

Colima

Inland, the capital of the small state of Colima is a charming city in a tropical setting, watched over jealously by two brooding volcanoes. Besides its colonial architecture, it has a fine Archaeological Museum (Museo de las Culturas de Occidente).

Puerto Vallarta

The major holiday resort on the Pacific coast after Acapulco,

Puerto Vallarta lies to the east of the immense bay of Banderas, which is, in fact, the edge of a submerged crater. Colonial-style houses are strewn over high, palm-covered slopes, all the way down to the shore hemmed with sandy white beaches.

With its red-tiled roofs and cobblestone streets, the centre, straddling the mouth of the Río Cuale river, has maintained an old-fashioned charm that has not been spoiled by the town's conversion to tourism. The shoreline is covered from one end to the other with hotel complexes, each one more luxurious than the last. To the north, past the marina and golf course, you reach the most recent holiday developments in Nuevo Vallarta. To the south, as far as Mismaloya, you'll find the prettiest beaches of the area.

Offshore, the national marine park centred around the rocky islets of Los Arcos is an internationally renowned centre for diving. Banderas bay, with its wealth of underwater fauna, is home to a large dolphin colony. The Marietas islands are known for their rock formations and the possibility (in spring) of spotting whales and manta rays.

Naturally, the full range of water sports are on offer here, too. The only problem is having to choose from the dozens of possibilities. Back on dry ground, there's golf, tennis, horse trekking—just about everything you can think of. Boat trips take you to Yelapa beach where you can dine to the soothing sound of the surf. Then set off for a nightclub, bar or discotheque; there are plenty to choose from in the city centre and the main hotels.

San Blas

In the days of New Spain, San Blas was an important stopover for the galleons sailing from the Philippines. Today nothing remains of its past save the ruins of an abandoned fort. Forgotten by history, this fishing village of colourful houses has remained practically unchanged. People now come here for the landscape of giant coconut palms, the spectacular beaches (Borrego and Matanchén) and excursions on the estuary: boats take you deep into the mangrove forest, home of all kinds of exotic birds.

Mazatlán

The northernmost of the Pacific beach resorts is also a major fishing port located on a peninsula. Activity centres around the beaches which stretch to the north for 15 km (9 miles) or so (Zona Dorada). Deep sea fishing is very popular here (marlin, sailfish, bonito, yellowfin tuna), as are the boat trips to desert islands inhabited by colonies of seabirds.

THE HIGH PLATEAUX

Guadalajara, Uruapan, Morelia

The Sierra Madre cuts through the states of Michoacán and Jalisco, at the western edge of the Altiplano. The Spaniards founded many cities on the wide plains, sheltered from the muggy tropical climate of the coast by the foothills, a refuge of Indian cultures.

Guadalajara

Its beginnings were fraught with difficulties. The city was finally established on its present site at the third attempt in 1542. Then there was no holding back: in 1560 Guadalajara became the capital of New Galicia—encompassing all the conquered territory west of Mexico City. Today, with almost 3 million inhabitants, it is Mexico's second city. Famous for its mariachis, its rodeos, its tequila and for the beauty of its women, the city embodies the strong Mexican identity in a setting of colonial architecture and refined elegance.

City Centre

Guadalajara's heart beats around a splendid group of four squares surrounding the cathedral, which was consecrated in 1616. This building features an unusual patchwork of styles, originally Gothic, and later embellished with baroque touches.

To the west, Plaza de los Laureles forms a front courtyard for the cathedral. It is bordered on the north by the Palacio Municipal. Plaza de los Hombres Illustres is a rotunda opening onto the regional museum housed in the Seminary of San José, with a flower-decked patio. The eclectic collections recall the history of the country from its early origins (mammoth skeletons) to colonial paintings.

Plaza de Armas, to the south, is the most pleasant of the squares. The Palacio de Gobernio (1774) displays a mixture of churriguresque and neoclassical styles. The central staircase has a dramatic mural by José Clemente Orozco, portraying Miguel Hidalgo proclaiming independence.

To the east, the Plaza de la Liberación, the largest of the four squares, is bordered by the Teatro Degollado, inaugurated in Maximilian's time. Nearby you will find the plateresque-style Palace of Justice and the Santa María de Gracia church, one of Guadalajara's earliest religious buildings.

Further on, past Plaza Tapatía, a large modern shopping complex, the Hospicio Cabañas is a former orphanage now housing a cultural centre known for its mural paintings by Orozco. The attractive, neoclassical building was inaugurated in 1810.

To the south, you will find all sorts of enticing goods in the Mercado Libertad, a large three-storey market. A passageway over Avenida Javier Mina takes you to the Plazuela de los Mariachis, in reality an alley bordered by restaurants and cafés where the famous musicians perform. Further on, to the southwest, the churches of Arazazu (churrigueresque) and San Francisco (baroque) are worth a detour. Continuing your stroll, you reach Agua Azul park, a large open area where the *tapatíos*, as the inhabitants of Jalisco state are called, can let off steam.

Zapopan

This suburb is the site of the 1730 Basilica of the Virgin of Zapopan, where a major pilgrimage takes place on October 4. A small Huichol Museum is devoted to this Indian people, among the most traditional in Mexico.

Heading towards Zacatecas, the road skirts the Barranca del Río de Santiago, a deep canyon plunging nearly 700 m (2,300 ft). There are good views from the zoo and the Parque Mirador.

Tlaquepaque

Southeast of Guadalajara, Tlaquepaque, with its pretty colonial architecture, has become a crafts centre especially renowned for its pottery. Here you find numerous galleries as well as a Ceramics Museum.

Further along, on the road to Mexico City, Tonalá is the site where many of the objects on sale in Tlaquepaque are produced, in particular the little animal figurines. A large market is held there on Thursdays and Sundays.

Uruapan

Founded in 1533 by a Franciscan monk, Uruapan is a small city with a pleasant colonial centre,

MARIACHIS

A reminder of more genteel times, when French was the language of style and elegance and couples were married to the sound of romantic serenades, the *mariachi* (from the local prnunciation of the French "mariage") originated in Guadalajara. These ear-splitting musicians in the fancy dress of the *charros*—gentlemen cowboys—have become the symbol of Mexican music. In the States of Jalisco and Michoacán alone there are more than 50,000, who can be hired by the hour or by the song. Three guitars, two violins and a couple of trumpets set the tone for romantic ballads and macho ditties.

Fields of agave paint the land blue: the core of the plant provides the basis of the national drink, tequila.

where the Chapel of La Guatapera and a Museum of Folk Art (traditional lacquerware) are outstanding. The Eduardo Ruiz national park, at the source of the Río Cupatitzio river, is a spacious garden of lush vegetation. The same river takes a plunge of some 20 m (65 ft) at the spectacular waterfalls of Tzararacua, 10 km (6 miles) to the south.

Paricutín

On February 20, 1943, a peasant was tilling the soil when he suddenly noticed a quivering mound of earth in front of his plough. It swelled up like a blister, and within a few hours started spewing forth smoke, rocks then lava. A week later, the unfortunate farmer's *milpa* (field) was buried beneath a 300-m (984-ft) volcano. Its successive eruptions eventually swallowed up two villages, including Paricutín, after which the volcano is named. Curious tourists flocked to see the spectacle and an observation post was built. Then, as suddenly as it had appeared, the volcano dried up. Today, Paricutín, 900 m (2950 ft) high, is a forlorn cone. The lonely clocktower of a buried church pokes up from the surrounding field of solidified lava.

The most popular tour involves riding on horseback to the crater from Angahuan, which, incidentally, has a noteworthy plateresque church built in 1562.

Pátzcuaro

Located at more than 2100 m (6890 ft) in a scenic mountain landscape, the large town of Pátzcuaro, on the shores of a superb lake, happily combines Spanish architecture and Indian atmosphere. The region is the homeland of the Tarascan Indians, a people of unknown origin who appeared here around the beginning of the 12th century.

Stroll along the cobblestone alleys bordered by low red and white houses with tile roofs. In the centre, colonial buildings enclose Plaza Vasco de Quiroga—named after a bishop who contributed to Pátzcuaro's fortune—with fountain and ancient trees. The Casa del Gigante, opposite the Palacio Municipal, and the Casa de los Once Patios, a former hospital, are striking examples of the local architecture. For a general view of all the local craft specialities, visit the Museum of Folk Arts, housed in a building dating from 1540. The Basilica of Nuestra Señora de la Salud, started by Bishop Quiroga, was originally planned to hold 30,000 faithful. After standing unfinished for years, it was finally completed in the 19th century on a more realistic scale.

To the west, Plaza Bocanegra, with its library, theatre and crafts market, retains an attractive colonial appearance. A bit further on you come to the lively hustle and bustle of the main market of Pátzcuaro.

A stone's throw from here is the shimmering azure lake. Some thirty traditional villages are dotted around its shores, and in the middle are three islands occupied by fishermen. Using big but-

TEQUILA

The town of Tequila, 50 km (30 miles) west of Guadalajara, is the production centre of Mexico's national tipple. The Sauza and Cuervo distilleries welcome visitors.

The making of tequila starts with the core of the *maguey*, or blue agave, which is chopped, steamed and then fermented for 36 hours to 3 days, before being distilled and aged in pine casks. Another variety of the same plant provides the raw material for *mezcal* (distilled), while the residue of the maguey is fermented and made into *pulque*, which has been drunk with gusto in Mexico since the earliest times. The Aztec deified it under 400 different forms, and only the elders were allowed to drink it.

terfly-shaped nets, they catch the prized *pescado blanco*, reputedly among the tastiest fish in the world.

The island of Janitzio, dominated by an ugly monument to Morelos, the champion of independence, has lost none of its peaceful charm. On the night of November 1 to 2, its cemetery is the scene of one of the most famous Festivals of the Dead in the country.

On the eastern shore of the lake, the hamlet of Tzintzuntzan, the old Tarascan capital, watches over the ruins of five circular temples *(yucatas)*, of which two have been restored. There is also a Franciscan monastery (1570) whose atrium is planted with ancient olive trees.

Morelia

Founded in 1541, the Michoacán state capital is perhaps the most Spanish of Mexico's cities. The churches and palaces of *tezontle* stone in the centre of Morelia seem to have been untouched by the ravages of time.

Constructed over more than 100 years, starting in 1640, the cathedral overlooks an enchanting Zócalo graced by laurel trees and enclosed by arcades. Facing it, the 17th-century Palacio de Gobierno contains murals on historical themes. On the other side of the square, the museum, in a baroque palace (1775), boasts a major collection of pre-Columbian objects, as well as paintings. Two other museums are devoted to the patriot, Morelos.

Northwest of the Zócalo, Avenida Madero leads to the college of San Nicolás de Hidalgo, founded in 1580. A little further up, on Calle Nigromante, the church of Santa Rosa has a magnificent baroque façade looking out onto a charming square. Notice the Palacio de Clavijero (1660) opposite, now housing a library. Next door is the Mercado de Dulces Regionales, a confectioners' market where you can indulge in candied fruit, a local speciality. Then investigate the interesting archaeological and historical collections at the State Museum of Michoacán, 176 Calle G. Prieto.

North of the Zócalo, you can reach the museum of colonial art via Plaza del Carmen. The House of Culture, with its interesting museum of masks, is also worth a visit.

To the east, in a former cloister of the San Francisco church (*azulejos*-tiled cupola) on Plaza Valladolid, the State Crafts Centre displays and sells delightful objects from all over the region.

On the limits of the city centre stands an 18th-century aqueduct. At one end is the Tarascan Fountain, floodlit at night.

BAJÍO

Querétaro, San Miguel de Allende, Guanajuato, San Luis Potosí, Real de Catorce, Zacatecas

In the centre of Mexico, the plain of Bajío ("low lands") is in fact located on the high plateau, at an altitude ranging from 1,500 to 1,800 m (4,920–5,900 ft). The breadbasket of the nation, it was long its major source of wealth: the discovery of rich silver deposits there in 1548 sparked an unprecedented silver rush, which led to colossal fortunes and fabulous cities. The Bajío later came to be known as the cradle of independence, leading to the birth of modern Mexico.

Querétaro

The second city of the region after San Luis Potosí, and growing at a tremendous pace, the historical capital of the Bajío has managed to preserve numerous traces of its turbulent past. In this city the first plot for independence was hatched in 1810; here Mexico renounced its sovereignty over Texas in 1848; Maximilian was shot here in 1867; and the Constitution still in force today was adopted here in 1917.

Old Centre

Streets lined with old Creole houses, shaded plazas, baroque churches—nothing much has changed in the old district. Begin your visit in the main square, Jardín Obregón. Several buildings of the former convent of San Francisco, founded in 1540, have been reconverted into a regional museum (paintings and objects from colonial times). There's also a beautiful church, its dome covered in *azulejos,* and Renaissance cloisters.

Behind the church is a pedestrian street which takes you to the Casa de la Corregidora—today the Palacio de Gobierno—famous for once having served as an improvised prison for the mayor's wife. Privy to the plot which was to bring about Mexico's independence, she nevertheless managed to get word out to her friends to warn them of the imminent danger of arrest. The nearby Plaza Independencia, with its arcades and stone-balconied houses, has a distinct Spanish flavour.

The church of San Antonio stands north of Jardín Obregón, together with the Teatro de la República, where Maximilian was sentenced to death. Take time to wander through the district, with its varied architecture: the neoclassical Neptune Fountain, plateresque and churriguresque church of Santa Clara, plateresque and baroque San Agustín church, and the Casa de los Peros with its weird gargoyles. The Museum of Art, on Calle Allende, is devoted to painting from the 16th to 20th centuries.To the southwest, the church of Santa Rosa (1752) is smothered in gold and marble.

Well to the east of the Zócalo, the Convent of the Cross, whose first stone was laid in 1654, offers a glimpse of the daily life of the nuns in the days of New Spain. A little further is a colonial aqueduct, still in use.

San Miguel de Allende

This adorable little colonial town is officially listed as a national monument. Houses painted in pastel colours cluster along its cobblestone streets against a hilly backdrop. The special quality of the light has attracted many artists to San Miguel, and its language schools cater to increasing numbers of students. Seduced by the easy-going lifestyle, a large permanent community of Americans has settled in the town, lending it a cosmopolitan atmosphere.

Town Centre

Plaza de Allende is the relaxing centre of town, with inviting park benches at the foot of old homes of nobles. Couples meet here, and the old folks gather to pass the time. The parish church *(parroquia)* is a Gothic jewel. The story goes that its façade was designed by an Indian mason, inspired by a postcard of Chartres cathedral in France. But the postcard only showed the front, and so the back of the building is very plain. Nearby there's a historical museum, the Casa de los Perros with its balcony supported on sculpted dogs, and the Casa del Mayorazgo de Canal, one of the most outstanding buildings in San Miguel.

Northeast of the Zócalo, heading towards San Francisco church with its handsome churriguresque façade, you will notice several other interesting buildings. The Oratorio de San Felipe Neri, beyond, has an intriguing baroque façade incorporating Indian influences.

It would take some time to see all of the town's churches. But don't miss La Salud, for its churriguresque portal, and La Concepción for the altar, altarpieces and dome, said to be modelled on that of the Invalides in Paris. Also noteworthy are the Prison of the Inquisition (Calle Cuadrante) and the Allende Institute (Calle Ancha de San Antonio), the former residence of the Count of Canal and now a highly reputed school of fine arts.

A serious contestant for the best balcony competition in San Miguel.

The Convent of Atotonilco, 15 km (9 miles) from San Miguel, is the focus of a major pilgrimage. Its walls are covered in frescoes.

Guanajuato

In an arid, mountainous region bristling with cactus, Guanajuato is the masterpiece of colonial Mexico. It looks as though it never crossed the gateway into the 20th century, with a haphazard maze of alleyways, staircases and underground passages that sprouted in whatever direction the town's mining activities took them. The town still seems to be living in its heady days as Mexico's Silver Capital. A homesick conquistador's dream, it harbours the vision of a long-lost Spain. Even Don Quixote haunts the streets: every November Guanajuato holds a joyous Cervantes Festival, in honour of the errant knight's creator.

Old Town

In the late afternoon, the strumming of guitars will guide you to the charming Jardín de la Unión. Here you can see the Teatro Juárez, inaugurated by President Porfirio Díaz, and the churrigueresque church of San Diego. A short walk to the west, La Paz square is enhanced by the 18th-century residences of the silver barons. It is dominated by the basilica of Nuestra Señora de Guanajuato, which contains an 8th-century wood sculpture of the Virgin presented by Philip II of Spain in 1557.

Overlooking it all is the University, a modern building well-integrated with the surrounding architecture, with three museums of art and a natural history collection. Next door is the imposing Compañía church (1747) and the Museo del Pueblo (folk arts and paintings), housed in the former residence of the marquises of San Juan de Rayas (1696). Further west, on Calle Pocitos, the birthplace of Diego Rivera has been turned into a museum.

Down from Plazuela de los Angeles, a tangled network of narrow alleyways clings to the hillside. In Callejón del Beso (Alley of the Kiss), the houses are so close together that apparently two lovers could kiss, each from their own balcony.

La Alhóndiga

Continue down Avenida Juárez, past the Hidalgo market below the Alhóndiga de Granaditas—a massive fortress converted into a historical museum. On the walls you can still see the hooks where the severed heads of supporters of indepence were displayed from 1811 to 1821.

Further on, the cemetery contains a rather unsettling museum. When they were clearing the

An intangible charm permeates the narrow streets of Guanajuato.

graves of those whose families could not pay for life concessions, the gravediggers discovered that the bodies were still intact. Thus, the macabre Museo del Panteon displays 107 mummies with their original clothes.

The Environs

The Pípila monument affords a peerless panorama over the town and mountains. To reach it by car, follow Calle Hidalgo, which runs along the dry bed of a diverted river.

Facing you, in the background, La Valenciana hill is riddled with galleries, from which several tonnes of precious metals are mined annually. For more than 200 years, it produced 20 per cent of the world's silver. You can visit the shafts, 500 m (1,640 ft) below ground, but your time may be better spent admiring the church of La Valenciana. A spectacular baroque confection, it was financed by the owner of the mine to thank Providence for his good fortune.

At the end of the 17th century the heirs of La Valenciana mine built the Hacienda San Gabriel Barrera in Marfil. Tastefully restored, its gardens and pergolas lead you to imagine the sumptuous lifestyle of some of the wealthiest Creole families.

San Luis Potosí

Capital of the state of the same name, San Luis stands on a barren plateau interspersed with clusters of cactus and patches of irrigated farmland. In the town centre, San Luis retains traces of its mining past, though its fortunes never equalled those of its namesake Potosí in Bolivia (site of the richest silver deposits in the world).

City Tour

The city is arranged around the Plaza de Armas, the *Potosinos*' favourite gathering place. To the east is the baroque cathedral and the town hall and, facing it, the neoclassical government building. On Calle Aldama, the old treasury, Antigua Caja Real, is an attractive building with typical balconies. Plaza de los Fundadores is the site of the church of La Compañía (1675), the Loreto chapel and the University, with its archaeological museum).

Southwest of the Zócalo is a baroque church watching over the peaceful Plaza San Francisco. The regional museum, housed in a former 16th-century Franciscan monastery, has collections of pre-Hispanic antiquities (principally Huastec) and, upstairs, the exuberant chapel of Aranzara, from the end of the 18th century.

To the east, heading towards Alameda park, other sites are grouped near Plaza del Carmen: the church of the same name, with its finely crafted churrigueresque façade, the neoclassical Teatro de la Paz, and the Museo Nacional de la Máscara, whose display of folkloric and ritual masks from all over the country should not be missed.

Real de Catorce

If Real de Catorce is not exactly a ghost town, it's the nearest thing to it. The city's only link to the outside world is a 3-km (2-mile) tunnel. Around 1780, a wander-

3

THE THREE MOST ATTRACTIVE COLONIAL TOWNS Mexico's silver cities are packed with memories of past splendour: Near the mines which brought riches to New Spain are timeworn palaces, rococo theatres and gilded altars, bringing back to mind a vanished Eldorado. **Guanajato**, a colonial pearl set in an arid valley; **Real de Catorce**, possessed by the ghosts of the glorious silver rush days; **Taxco**, the domes of its churches swathed in the mist from the hills.

ing Indian minstrel stumbled on a vein of silver in this forsaken corner of the mountains. He immediately rushed off to register his claim under the name of "Our Lord of the Miracles". The resulting silver rush transformed Real de Catorce—despite its inaccessible location in a barren mountain basin at 2,800 m (9,185 ft)—into a city of 30,000 inhabitants. At the peak of its glory, it boasted a theatre, a bullring, a pit for cockfights and even a tramway. The main square still has its rococo street lamps. The Casa de la Moneda, opposite the parish church, minted its own coins in the 1860s.

Flooding and exhaustion of the silver veins brought about Real de Catorce's decline. At its lowest ebb, the population was reduced to 27 inhabitants. It has now increased to around 1,200, but the community has barely caught up with the 20th century.

Zacatecas

Situated at 2,500 m (8,200 ft) in a landscape of arid mountains, Zacatecas winds around a large crag, the Cerro de la Bufa. Before the Conquest, the Indians were already mining the rich silver deposits here. Then the conquistadors arrived and here, in the middle of the desert, blossomed one of the great architectural achievements of Mexico.

The centre clusters around Plaza de Hidalgo and the baroque cathedral, a masterpiece of religious art. Apart from the façade, note the towers, typical examples of churriguresque style. The Palacio de Gobierno (1727) opposite used to belong to one of the silver barons. The handsome Teatro Calderón stands next to the market, very lively in the morning.

West of the cathedral, a street climbs to the sober baroque church of Santo Domingo. The buildings of the former Jesuit college (don't miss the attractive cloisters) now house the Pedro Coronel Museum, where the artist's private collection is on display.

A maze of uneven cobblestone streets stretches southwards. Musicians gather for outdoor evening performances in front of San Agustín church.

Northwest of the city centre, El Edén mine, today a museum, provided almost a quarter of all Mexican silver at the beginning of the 18th century. A guide will take you into the dark galleries, first in a mine cart, then over creaking planks. In colonial times, work conditions practically amounted to slavery and took a toll of 3,000 Indian lives every year.

For a panoramic view of the city, take the cable car to the eyrie of La Bufa, crowned by a little shrine (1728).

ARTESANIAS
Victoria

THE NORTH

Chihuahua, Sierra Tarahumara

Far from the pyramids of the old empires and the golden beaches of the Pacific lies yet another Mexico: 2,000 km (1,240 miles) of desolate plains, rugged sierras, bottomless canyons, an occasional oasis, and millions of saguaro cactuses, branched like candelabra. Dominated by the Sonora Desert, this is the Mexico of westerns and of Pancho Villa. It's just like the films, with pueblos shimmering in the sweltering heat and *vaqueros* (cowboys) driving their herds down to the river bank. The Indians, descendants of Geronimo's tribe, tend to keep to themselves. Secluded in their valleys, they avoid contact with the outside world.

Chihuahua

Hatted and booted and clinking their spurs, cowboys stroll in style along the wide avenues of Chihuahua, capital of Mexico's biggest state. The sprawling ranches of the region still belong to the descendants of the handful of families who owned half the state at the beginning of the 20th century. Then along came Pancho Villa, a peasant's son, and the Revolution. Today the region is rich, thanks to livestock breeding but also to its proximity to the US: subsidiaries of American factories represent Mexico's second-largest source of foreign revenue.

The centre of the city, at the foot of a pretty baroque cathedral, is not uninteresting, but most visitors head straight for the Quinta Luz, one-time home of Pancho Villa and now the Museo de la Revolución. Here you'll discover all the equipment of a perfect revolutionary: pistols, swords, bandoleers, and also a collection of rare photographs from the period. Several rooms are devoted to the history of the Revolution, and in the garden you can see the bullet-riddled antediluvian Dodge in which Villa was assassinated.

Creel: gateway to the secretive world of the Tarahumara Indians.

Sierra Tarahumara

In 13 hours, the Chihuahua al Pacífico railway covers almost 650 km (400 miles) through a dramatic landscape of high plains sliced by grandiose *barrancas*—inaccessible sunken canyons. The track glides through the pine-covered foothills of the Sierra Madre, winding over no less than 39 bridges and through 86 tunnels. Started in 1898, the railway was not finished until 1961, at the expense of tremendous effort.

A truly legendary train, the Chihuahua al Pacífico boasts picture windows, one steward per carriage and seats that swivel round so you don't have to travel backwards. If you leave from Chihuahua, you'll get the best view from the seats on the left-hand side (daily departure at 7 a.m.; reservation advisable).

Creel

The train stops at this little lumber town high up in the mountains at an altitude of 2,345 m (7,694 ft). Creel is the departure point for numerous excursions. You can hire a horse for a ride to the Arareco Lake or to the Cusárare waterfall, which plunges 30 m (100 ft). You can also visit the more remote falls at Basaseáchic (245 m; 800 ft). But the town is, above all, the gateway to the closed world of the Tarahumara Indians. A footpath takes you to the caves at the base of cliffs where some of their communities live.

El Divisadero

At an altitude of 2,250 m (7,382 ft), the train reaches the Barranca del Cobre (Copper Canyon) for a 30-minute stop. Some reckon that the Grand Canyon would fit inside it, with room to spare. The vertiginous vista sweeps from the forested heights into a seemingly bottomless chasm. Down below where the *río* flows, tropical vegetation flourishes. If you want to go there, count a full day's journey by mule. If half an hour is all you can spare, have a look at the handicrafts on display, made by the Indians. Should you wish to linger a while, El Divisadero provides a good base for further exploration of the region.

Around Batopilas, *Chiveadores* are still prospecting for that elusive gold.

PANCHO VILLA

Also known as Francisco Villa, but originally Doroteo Arango, Pancho Villa (1878–1923) was the leader of a band of outlaws, a sort of Mexican Robin Hood. At 33, he joined the Revolution, recruited an army of *peones* (farm labourers), became master of the countryside and later of Chihuahua. He led raids into US territory to obtain provisions, unleashing the wrath of the Americans, who sent a detachment under General Pershing in a futile attempt to capture him, in 1916. Villa finally agreed to abandon politics. He was pardoned in 1920 but ambushed and killed in Parral three years later. Mourned by 22 wives and countless offspring, he embodies Mexico's struggle against injustice.

BAJA CALIFORNIA

Northern Baja California, Southern Baja California

About 10 million years ago, violent earthquakes along the San Andreas fault ripped through the Pacific coast of northern Mexico. In a preview of the Big One which some day could strike further north, the earth was torn asunder and the ocean rushed in to fill the gap. Thus was born Baja California—or La Baja, as American visitors call it—a peninsula 1,200 km (895 miles) long, and 100 km (60 miles) wide.

With 2,500 km (1,550 miles) of coastline, La Baja is above all a marine wonderland. Since the 1980s, its endless beaches have sparked a boom in tourism. But once you venture inland, the desert reigns supreme. A succession of mountain ranges forms a backbone to the land, in places flat and monotonous, in others deeply scarred by gorges and valleys. And everywhere there are cactuses, growing in a multitude of shapes and sizes. The largest, the *cirio*, can reach a height of 20 m (65 ft).

The peninsula was neglected for hundreds of years. Only the missionaries, led by the Jesuits, forged stubbornly on. They left behind the region's only treasures: dozens of missions they named after saints. Apart from that, the land was left to the cowboys. Big city guys would scathingly remark to the handful of locals: "Why don't you try planting clouds?"

Northern Baja California

Before 1973, visiting the peninsula was almost impossible. Then the Mexican government, aware of the area's potential for tourism, endeavoured to put an end to its isolation. The resulting highway, the Carretera Transpeninsular, runs from Tijuana, on the US border, to Cabo San Lucas, at the southern tip of the peninsula.

Tijuana

Along a dozen city blocks on each side of Avenida Revolución, rows of *cantinas*, cabarets and discotheques do honour to the avenue's reputation as "the longest bar in the world". Americans have patronized the saloons of Tijuana since the turn of the century. In the 1920s, the number of bars multiplied. With Prohibition in force on the other side of the border, the town went mad. The pace is still frenetic: every year, 25 million foreign visitors throng to the buzzing town centre. But Tijuana is not as dissolute as its reputation would have it. The dens of sin have given way to souvenir shops, selling everything from cowboy boots to outsize sombreros.

With nearly 2 million inhabitants, the city is looking to the future: the economic boom has given rise to an outbreak of skyscrapers, and the University is one of the most prestigious in the country. Near the *río*, the Cultural Centre bears witness to the city's new aspirations.

Ensenada and beyond

For the first 100 km (60 miles), the Transpeninsular follows the coast and its glorious beaches to Ensenada, the largest fishing port in Mexico. Great crowds gather there at the weekend. In the neighbourhood, you can visit the Bodegas of Santo Tomás which produce one of the best wines in La Baja.

Near San Quintín, 300 km (200 miles) further on, the first cactuses come into view. In Rosario de Arriba you cross the threshold of an imaginary frontier as the road leaves the coast. After Cataviña, branch off the main road for Bahía de los Angeles, a popular fishing spot. Inland, the shrine of San Francisco de Borja is the best preserved of the region's adobe missions. Just before the road reaches Guerrero Negro, an enormous monument marks the 28th parallel, and the gateway to the Vizcaíno Desert.

4

THE FOUR MOST COLOURFUL FIESTAS The fiestas combine religious fervour with an unbridled festive spirit. Indian by nature, they revolve around the more magical aspects of life. The Christian **Semana Santa** is an excuse for ancestral tribal dances, or jigs inherited from the Spanish conquest: the Zapatec Feather Dance, the Tarahumara dances of the Deer or the Turkey. On October 4, the peasants of Cuetzalán don colourful costumes and bright plumage for the **Dance of the Quetzals**. For the **Feast of the Dead**, All Saint's Day, in Mixquic and on the island of Janitzio in Pátzcuaro Lake, the shops are full of sugar skulls, and hordes of papier-mâché skeletons join the parade. On December 12, the **Feast of the Virgin of Guadalupe**, patron saint of Mexico, is the climax of pilgrimages spread over a week, and the Dance of the Volador is performed in Huehuetla, in the Sierra de Puebla.

Southern Baja California

The maritime character of the peninsula becomes more apparent in the southern half of the peninsula.

Guerrero Negro

This region boasts the largest salt marshes in the world. Five million tonnes of the purest salt are harvested annually—a reminder of the times when working the salt marshes was the only activity tolerated by the Spaniards. The wide lagoon, Ojo de Liebre (also called Scammon's Lagoon), is a major breeding area for the grey whale: they come here to give birth in the warm waters after a journey of 10,000 km (6,000 miles). Far offshore, the island of Cedro and the islets of San Benitos are home to colonies of sea lions and elephant seals.

The oases

Once again the road leaves the coast to plunge into the Vizcaíno desert. San Ignacio is a little oasis blessed with a large palm grove planted by the Jesuits and a mission built of basalt (1786).

Hidden away in the heart of the desolate Sierra de San Francisco is one of the treasures of Baja California: prehistoric paintings etched on the walls of large caves, portraying men and large animals. From San Ignacio or San Francisco, a guide will lead you by mule to the Cueva del Ratón (the most accessible of the caves) or the superb Cueva Pintada, at the bottom of the San Pablo canyon.

Sea of Cortés

In Santa Rosalía, a small port where the French traded in copper until the 1950s, do not miss the iron church designed by Gustave Eiffel (he of the tower). It found its way to Baja California towards the end of the 19th century in parts, apparently shipped there by mistake.

The wide bays where English pirates hid out in the 18th century spread their sandy beaches at the end of a bumpy track. Offshore, the gulf harbours an exceptionally rich marine life, and the area is home to colonies of spectacular aquatic birds. The town of Mulegé nestles on the bay of La Concepción, often considered the most striking of them all. There's a small mission (1705) here, and an oasis of date palms.

Founded in 1697, Loreto was the first capital of Baja California. It also boasts a mission, magnificently restored, and a museum tracing the ethnographic history of the settlement.

To the south, Nopoló and Puerto Escondido are staking everything on tourism: now a centre for game fishing, the coast has been

equipped with hotel complexes, golf courses and marinas.

The Transpeninsular leaves the coast again for the 300-km (200-mile) cross-country stretch to La Paz. From Ciudad Constitución, a well-maintained road leads to Magdalena Bay on the Pacific, famous for its large colony of whales that winter here.

La Paz

Capital of southern Baja California, La Paz was one of the world's principal centres of the pearling industry in the 18th century. From those distant times, the city has retained a colonial centre and, of course, its superb natural harbour. With a new lease of life as a holiday resort, La Paz is dedicated to diving and fishing. You can spend lazy days on the beaches of the Pichilingue peninsula or strolling along the seaside promenade of the Malecón, with every evening an invariably spectacular sunset.

Southern Tip

Just before it reaches San José del Cabo, the road crosses the Tropic of Cancer, marked by a globe-shaped monument.

At the southernmost tip of Baja California, the tourist boom has transformed the little port of San José into a latter-day Eldorado. Boats have been adapted for deep-sea fishing, and the beaches are hemmed by hotels. Even so the heart of the town remains its traditional self, with narrow alleys and a small, shaded Zócalo.

Cabo San Lucas, 30 km (20 miles) to the west, has all you could possibly ask of a luxury beach resort. People come here for the beaches, the diving, and the fishing. The waters of the Pacific mingle with those of the Sea of Cortés. Take a trip beyond the cliffs to an arch of rock sculpted by the waves, sheltering the beach of Playa del Amor where you'll feel as if you have reached the end of the world.

WHALES

Each year from Christmas to the end of March, thousands of grey whales take over the sheltered bays of Baja California: Ojo de Liebre, Magdalena, San Ignacio. The warm, shallow waters here are ideal for giving birth to the calves. When the baby whales are strong enough, the lengthy return journey to the Arctic begins. Long threatened with extinction, the whales are now fully protected and have built up their numbers to more than 15,000.

In the desert, cacti grow to spectacular heights.

GULF OF MEXICO

El Tajín, Jalapa, Zempoala, Veracruz, Villahermosa

On the eastern slopes of the Mexican plateaux, the wide tropical plain of Tierras Calientes borders the Gulf of Mexico. In the north lies the Totonac territory. In the south, the Olmecs shaped the "mother culture", the origin of Meso-American civilization.

El Tajín

The Pyramid of El Tajín, one of the finest in Mexico, is the masterpiece of the Totonac civilization. Little is known about the origins of the city and its builders, who reached their period of greatest splendour between the 7th and 9th centuries. It would appear that the fundamental elements of the Totonac religion were an obsession with death and a devotion to the ritual ball game.

The Ruins

The site nestles among several forested hillocks, some of which are in fact unexcavated buildings. Especially well preserved, the pyramid of Los Nichos, 20 m (65 ft) high, has six tiers, each topped with diminishing numbers of niches. Those of the upper temple have been destroyed, but archaeologists have calculated that there were initially 365 niches, corresponding to the number of days in the solar year. The pyramid may have served as some sort of giant calendar. The niches were originally painted red inside, with blue frames. The neighbouring constructions, arranged around a square, follow a similar design.

The southern ball court is the largest of El Tajín's total of eleven. It is 60 m (196 ft) long, and the walls are decorated with 12th-century bas-reliefs portraying ritual scenes, the best-known of which shows the sacrifice of a player.

To the north, Plaza de El Tajín Chico encompasses the old administrative centre of the city. Near the entrance there is a small museum.

Volador

Every weekend between 11 a.m. and 1 p.m., and occasionally on weekdays, Totonac dancers re-enact the ceremony of the Volador: the leading dancer and his four partners, dressed in traditional costume, shin up to the top of a 20-m (65-ft) post topped by two tiny platforms. On the highest one, the leader dances a few steps to the sound of a flute and a drum. When he stops, the four *voladores* (fliers) hurl themselves into the air, with a rope attached to their waist or an ankle. As the rope plays out, they glide, their arms spreadeagled, in ever-increasing circles until they reach the ground.

The meaning of the Volador ritual has been lost in the mists of time, but it is generally thought to have started as some kind of fertility rite. The *voladores*, who might originally have worn bird costumes, represent the points of the compass, and the ritual would invoke rain or sunshine for the harvest. Under the Aztecs, this ceremony was linked to ritual sacrifice: a man was slain with arrows as part of the proceedings.

Jalapa

On the eastern edge of the upper plateau, the capital of the State of Veracruz is a fetching colonial city graced by numerous tropical gardens kept perpetually green by the *chipichipi*, a persistent drizzle. Its situation on a hill offers superb views over the coastal plain.

Visitors come to Jalapa to visit its Museum of Anthropology, the most interesting in the country after that of Mexico City. The magnificently designed building enhances the splendid archaeological displays within, devoted mainly to the Totonac and Olmecs. The museum features no less than 7 of the 16 colossal stone heads discovered to date, of which the most important, from San Lorenzo, is 2.70 m (nearly 9 ft) tall and weighs 16 tonnes. All depict expressionless faces with flat noses and thick lips.

Zempoala

Close to the spot where Hernán Cortés landed, Zempoala was the first city to ally itself with the Spaniards. The Totonac city, under the Aztec yoke since 1463, had 30,000 inhabitants at the time.

BALL GAME

No one knows who invented the game of *tlachtli*. But the Olmec (whose name in Náhuatl means "The Rubber People") already played it. The Totonac were mad about this combination of sport and ritual, and the Aztecs were also *tlachtli* fanatics. The court, shaped like an H, symbolized the cosmos, and the movement of the ball was meant to represent that of the sun. The ball had to be kept in constant motion, but it could only be passed around by using the knees and shoulders. The object of the game was to send the ball through a stone ring fixed to one of the walls. Legend has it that the captain of the losing team was put to death, though it may well have been, in fact, an honour reserved for the winning side.

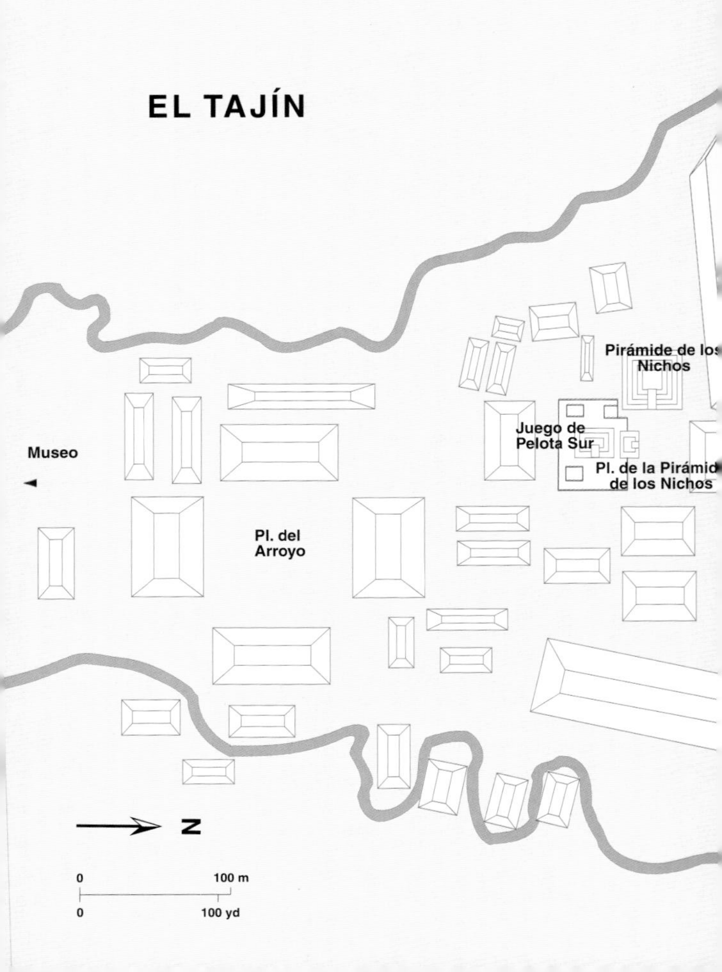
EL TAJÍN
Pirámide de los
Nichos
Juego de
Pelota Sur
Pl. de la Pirámid
de los Nichos
Museo
Pl. del
Arroyo
N
0
100 m
0
100 yd

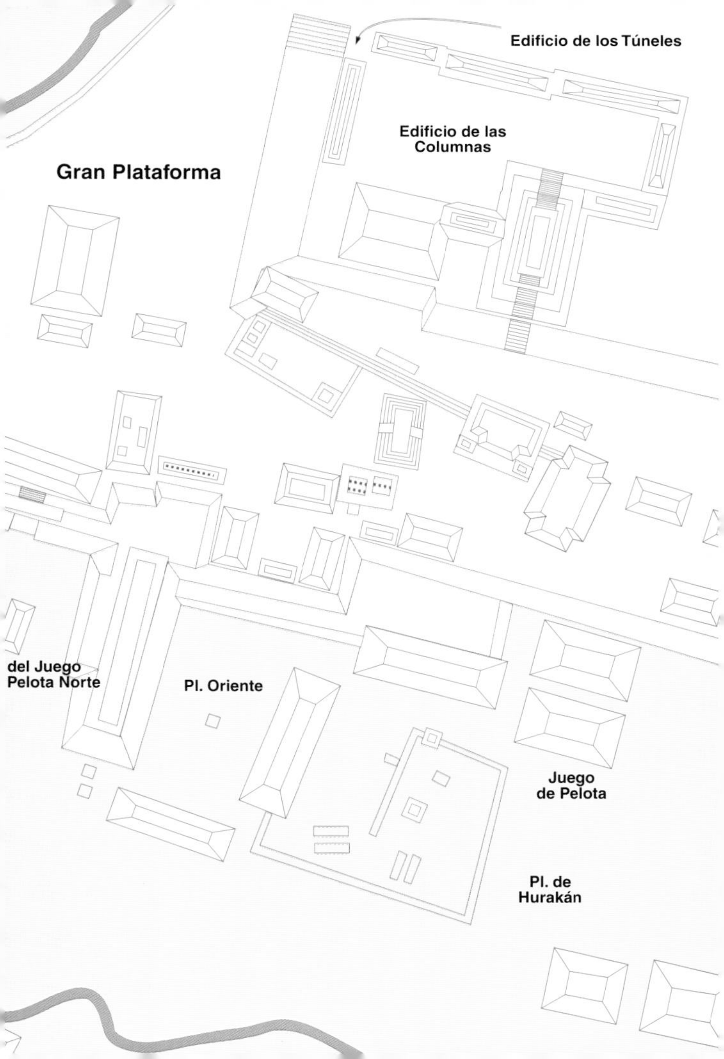

Edificio de los Túneles
Edificio de las Columnas
Gran Plataforma
del Juego
Pelota Norte
Pl. Oriente
Juego
de Pelota
Pl. de
Hurakán

VANILLA

The fragrant orchid, Vanilla planifolia, has been cultivated in the Tierras Calientes since pre-Hispanic times. The Aztecs were immensely fond of vanilla flavouring, and they controlled the region where the plant grew. It was later introduced to the Philippines by the Spaniards, and from there it became known to the rest of the world. Today, in Papantla, vanilla is sold as an extract (xanath), in crinkled black pods, or in figuras—the pods braided into floral or animal motifs.

The ruins are divided into twelve groups. The main one, within an enclosure, is that of the Templo Mayor. Apart from the principal temple, of Aztec inspiration, it includes the Templo de las Chimeneas (Chimneys) on a raised platform, and the Great Pyramid. To the east in the next enclosure, the Templo de Las Caritas ("Little Faces") is so named for the rows of inset clay skulls which adorned its interior walls, above symbols for the sun, moon and evening star.

At weekends, the Dance of the Volador ceremony is held at Zempoala.

Veracruz

Mexico's major port was for many years the country's hub of trade and its only link with the outside world. Cargoes of silk and porcelain from Asia, and gold and silver from the American colonies were unloaded at Acapulco on the Pacific coast, carried by mule train over the sierras, and re-loaded at Veracruz for shipping to Europe. The importance of the transactions attracted numerous pirates who even managed to capture and loot the city in 1683. In 1746 solid ramparts were constructed to defend the city and its port.

The Old Town

Though there's little to show, nowadays, of its former glory, Veracruz still has a certain charm, particularly in the region of its large Zócalo. One one side stands the town hall, restored several times since its construction in the 17th century, and on another, the parish church. Visitors and residents meet beneath the shade of its palm trees, and the place has a festive atmosphere that reaches boiling point during the Carnival, claimed to be "the biggest between New Orleans and Rio de Janeiro".

Of the nine bastions which stood along the city walls, only that of Santiago remains. To the north, the island of San Juan de

A colossal Olmec sculpted stone head was discovered in this marshy region near Santiago Tuxtla.

Ulúa, where Cortés landed in 1519, is now connected to the mainland. The chapel built in 1524 was replaced by one of the most notorious prisons in Mexico: its cells were flooded during spring tides.

Sierra de Los Tuxtlas

Southeast of Veracruz spreads a marshy landscape reminiscent of the Camargue in France, dotted with villages of brightly coloured houses. This region saw the first Olmec settlements. Lake Catemaco is a beautiful stretch of water surrounded by forest. The town of Catemaco on the western shore is known for its witch doctors.

Villahermosa

The capital of Tabasco state, fairly pleasant despite its modern outskirts, has an interesting museum (CICOM) dedicated to the Olmecs and Maya.

Near the airport, the Parque-Museo de La Venta was set up in the 1960s to provide a new home for finds excavated at the famous Olmec site of La Venta, set in the middle of the marshes some 100 km (60 miles) from here, in an area threatened by oil prospecting. The fabulous sculptures were relocated in this tropical park where you can also see stelae and carvings depicting animals and men.

INDIAN STATES AND SITES

Oaxaca, Chiapas, Palenque, Yaxchilán

In the southeast of Mexico, two states stand out in particular because of their pre-Columbian heritage: Oaxaca, in the heart of the Zapotec zone, a land of arid mountains, and Chiapas, ranging from cool to tropical; homeland of the Tzotzil and the Tzeltal, descendants of the Maya.

Oaxaca

Long before the Conquest, the Zapotec—or "Cloud People"—established one of the most brilliant civilizations of Meso-America, centred around the Oaxaca Valley. Together with the Mixtec, Mixe, Trique and several other indigenous peoples, they make up the most ethnically diverse state in Mexico. Nearly half of its 3 million inhabitants speak one of the 100 Indian dialects recorded in the region. This cultural diversity is a direct consequence of the unusual topography: splintered into hundreds of enclaves, the Sierra Madre harbours just as many distinct worlds.

The Capital

Oaxaca town, the administrative centre of the state, is a quintessential colonial city, an unambitious, easy-going place at the crossroads of Spanish architecture and Indian culture.

It is relatively small and can easily be visited on foot, especially as there are numerous pedestrian zones, starting with the district surrounding the wide Zócalo. Peaceful by day, the square gets livelier as evening progresses and the terraces and cafés start to fill up. On one side is the neoclassical Palacio de Gobierno, and on the other the cathedral, which is mainly interesting for its baroque façade. Next to the cathedral is the Alameda Park, near the 17th-century Compañía church. Unfortunately, the Juárez covered market has lost its picturesque atmosphere to the Abastos market, further from the centre.

Follow Calle Alcalá, past several handsome 17th- and 18th-century stone houses, to reach the striking baroque church of Santo Domingo. The adjacent convent now houses the State Museum. Here you can see collections of objects from Monte Albán, including a treasure trove discovered in a Mixtec tomb.

Other museums to visit here include Casa de Juárez, dedicated to the Zapotec-born president, and the Rufino Tamayo museum, the former home of the artist, now housing a magnificent collection of pre-Columbian statues.

The churches of San Felipe and La Soledad, along Avenida Independencia, are also well worth inspection.

To the northwest, the Cerro El Fortin is a forested hill offering a sweeping view over Oaxaca.

Monte Albán

On top of an esplanade built at an altitude of 2,000 m (6,560 ft), the Zapotec created a magnificent ceremonial city. Begun around 500 BC, Monte Albán is a patchwork of different cultural influences: Olmec for the first period, Maya for the second. In the third phase (4th–7th centuries), the Zapotec civilization reached its peak, developing strong links with Teotihuacán. A period of decline followed, until the arrival of the Mixtec who used the site as a necropolis for their dignitaries.

The buildings, most of them dating from the Zapotec period, are arranged around a large central square bounded by two raised platforms. You will see several temples, a palace, an observatory and a ball court. Note the Monument of the Dancers, so-called for the bas-reliefs portraying figures of the Olmec type.

To the north of the site there are many tombs, of which the most interesting (no. 104), dating from the 5th century, is covered in frescoes of Teotihuacán influence.

The Central Valleys

Three valleys converge at Oaxaca, an important crafts centre where the Indians come to sell their wares. However, it can be more rewarding to visit in person the Zapotec hamlets scattered among the mountains. Each jealously guards its own identity in its embroidery patterns or methods of working the land.

Teotitlán del Valle is one of the most famous weaving villages in Mexico. Santa Ana del Valle maintains a textile tradition that goes back to pre-Hispanic days. The most sought-after pottery comes from San Bartolo de Coyotepec. You'll make your best buys at the weekly markets, among the most colourful in the country: Tlacolula and Ayulta on Sundays, Zacatepec on Wednesdays, Zaachila on Thursdays, Ocotlán on Fridays, and so forth.

In addition to the deep-rooted traditional character of its people, the valleys of Oaxaca are also fascinating for their pre-Columbian sites, some 300 in all. Among the most important, Dainzú is famed for its stone slabs sculpted with figures of ball players; Lambityeco for its two patios covered in friezes; Yagul, on a cactus-covered hill, once one of the biggest Zapotec towns. Mitla, was both Zapotec and Mixtec and blends the two styles. The best-preserved architectural

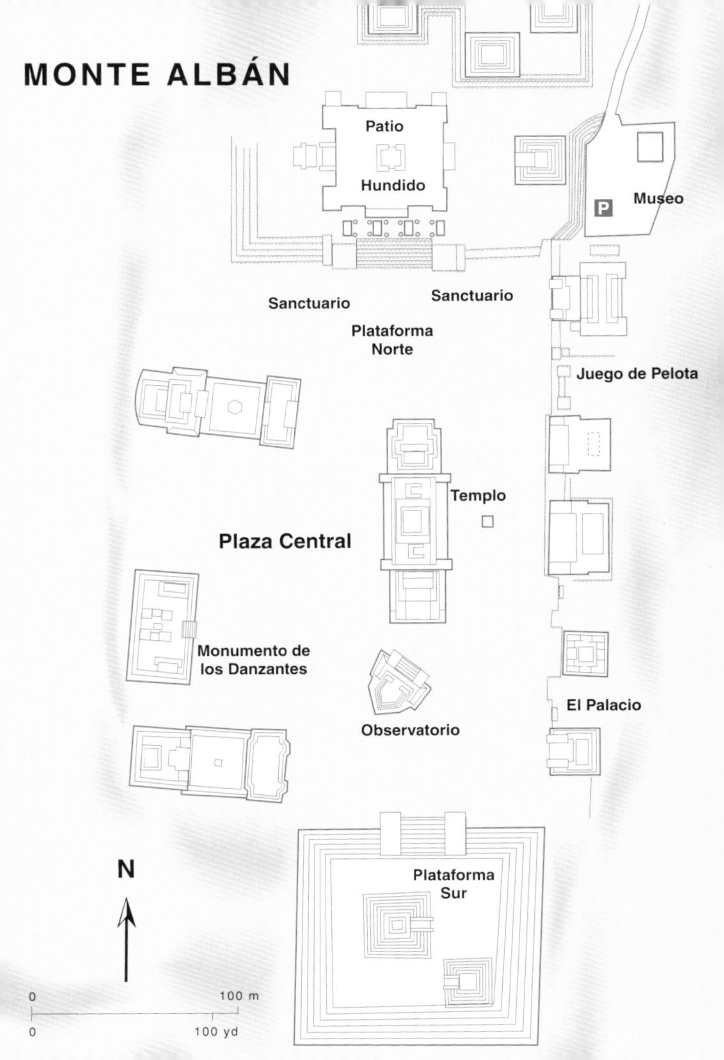
MONTE ALBÁN
Patio
Hundido
Museo
P
Sanctuario
Sanctuario
Plataforma
Norte
Juego de Pelota
Templo
Plaza Central
Monumento de
los Danzantes
Observatorio
El Palacio
Plataforma
Sur
N
0
100 m
0
100 yd

group—Grupo de las Columnas —includes a small courtyard known as the Patio de las Grecas, after the fretwork on its interior walls in the Greek key pattern.

Last but not least, Cuilapan, near Oaxaca, has the remains of a Dominican monastery (1555) with a remarkable Renaissance cloister.

Mixteca

The western part of the state is the homeland of the Mixtec, its second-largest group of Indians after the Zapotec. The region boasts three beautiful Christian religious buildings, a small distance from each other. At Yanhuitlán, the convent (1550) includes a church with a handsome plateresque façade. In Teposcolula, the Dominican monastery has an open chapel of the same style. The most impressive of all three, the monastery of Coixtlahuaca stands majestically on a raised platform.

Chiapas

This is Maya territory. Chiapas, a bewitching land of canyons, volcanoes and impenetrable jungle, is the home of the mysterious Tzotzils and the last of the Lacandon Indians. Heirs of a vanished civilization, they maintain ancient rites and beliefs. The jungle conceals the marvellous cities of their ancestors.

Dignified and discreet, the Indians of San Cristóbal keep to themselves.

Tuxtla Gutiérrez

The state capital is worth visiting if only for its Chiapas Museum, devoted to the region's archaeology and ethnology, with fine examples of Maya stelae and traditional costumes. There is also a zoo, where you can observe some of the local fauna more difficult to spot in situ (jaguars, pumas, macaws, etc). But Tuxtla is principally the gateway to the splendid Cañon del Sumidero, in some parts reaching up to 1,000 m (3,280 ft) deep. A road takes you to a number of lookout points offering incredible views over the gorge, the Río Grijalva and its banks, thickly overgrown. The old colonial village of Chiapa de Corzo, 16 km (10 miles) to the south, is known for its lacquered masks and gourds. From here, boat trips follow the river as far as the dam. On the way, you can spot all kinds of exotic birds and maybe a crocodile or two.

San Cristóbal de las Casas

The stylish colonial town of San Cristóbal, founded in 1528, is brimming with charm. Its elegant aristocratic mansions and simple tile-roofed houses cluster around

THE LACANDON

The 500-odd Lacandon Indians, scattered in the jungle of eastern Chiapas, are direct descendants of the Maya. They are loyal to the same gods as their ancestors: Balum, the jaguar, is the keystone of their religion. Now and then, some of the men will emerge from the forest to sell their bows and arrows at Palenque. But the construction of new roads, deforestation and the subsequent arrival of new immigrants is threatening the Lacandon way of life.

a Zócalo perfect for letting the hours drift by.

The town has a cathedral and numerous churches, but none can match the church of Santo Domingo, a superb example of baroque. Indian women sell their handicrafts on the courtyard in front of the church. The Tzotzil capital, San Cristóbal is a window opening onto a fascinating world of ancient customs. For a glimpse of the weaving techniques, visit the workshop of Sna Jolobil in the former Convent of Santo Domingo. The works on display, of high quality, are brought in from a score of villages in the region.

The nearby market is renowned throughout the country. The villagers turn up in their traditional costume. You'll easily recognize the inhabitants of Zinacantán by their pink tunics and flat hats festooned with ribbons, and those of San Juan Chamula by their cream-coloured *huipil* blouses.

For an Indian experience of a different sort, visit Casa Na-Bolom (33 Calle Vicente Guerrero), a small museum uniting the ethnographic collections of Maya expert Frans Blom, of Danish origin, and his widow Gertrude, a Swiss anthropologist and photographer, devoted to the Lacandon cause. Excellent photographs of the Tzotzil Indians are sold here.

Indian villages

Numbering some 150,000, the Tzotzil live in the craggy countryside within a radius of 50 km (30 miles) of San Cristóbal.

With San Cristóbal as your base, you can set forth to discover their scattered hamlets, each one clustered around a church where ritual Maya beliefs blend with Christian worship. Zinacantán and San Juan Chamula are high on the tourists' lists, especially during fiesta time. Though they are well accustomed to being invaded by curious visitors, the villagers do not take fondly to cameras, which in any case are banned in the churches and during religious ceremonies. You

The Palace at Palenque, and its intriguing tower.

might feel less of an intruder in more distant villages such as San Andrés Larraínzar or San Pedro Chenalhó. Tzotzil markets are held on Sunday mornings.

Lagunas de Montebello

Near the border with Guatemala, the national park is a jungle with some three score lakes of different colours, varying from the turquoise Laguna Agua and the bright green Laguna Esmeralda to the inky violet Agua Tinta.

To the west, the Maya site of Chinkultic, barely extricated from the encroaching jungle, looks out over other lakes and a *cenote*, a deep, natural well used as a place of sacrifice. A ball court spreads at the foot of a raised platform, which is, in turn, topped by a pyramid.

Palenque

Deep in the tropical forest that cloaks the rolling hills at the edge of the plain of Tabasco, Palenque is one of the most incredible sites in Mexico. Barely a tenth of the archaeological zone has been excavated: the Maya city is thought to have spread over an area of nearly 20 sq km (8 sq miles). All that we know of its history is that it saw its heyday from the beginning of the 7th to the end of the 8th century, mainly under the

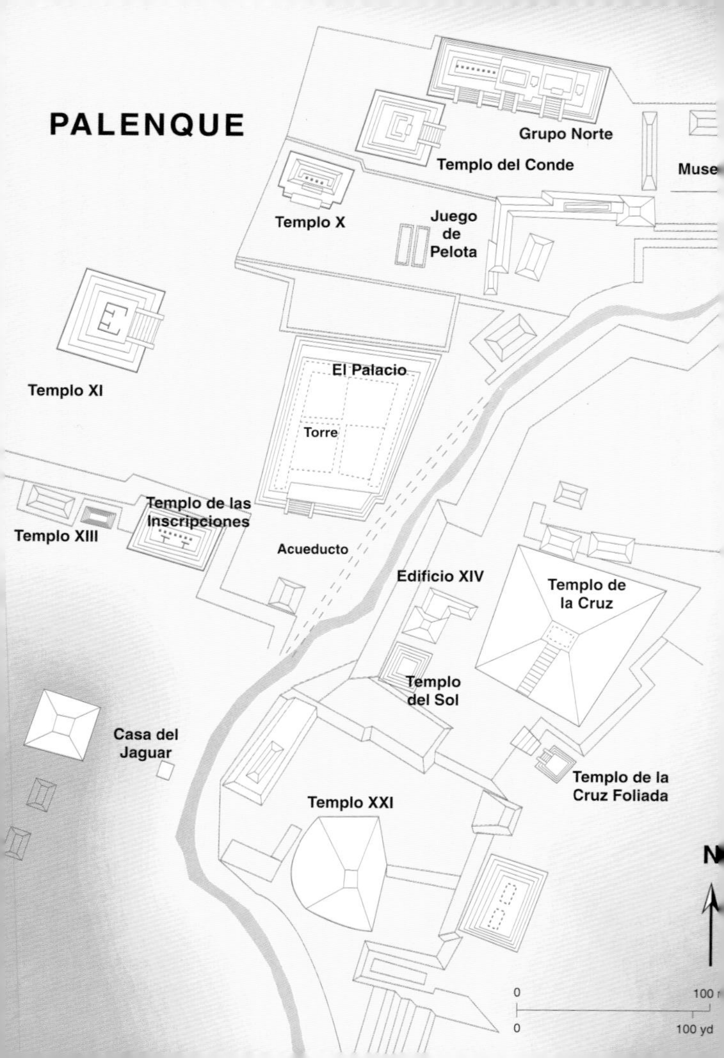

PALENQUE
Grupo Norte
Templo del Conde
Muse
Templo X
Juego
de
Pelota
Templo XI
El Palacio
Torre
Templo de las
Inscripciones
Templo XIII
Acueducto
Edificio XIV
Templo de
la Cruz
Templo
del Sol
Casa del
Jaguar
Templo de la
Cruz Foliada
Templo XXI
N
0
100
0
100 yd

reign of Kin Pakal (Shield of the Sun) and his son, Chan-Balum, the Serpent-Jaguar.

Temple of the Inscriptions

It was they who ordered the construction of the majority of the buildings, including this temple at the top of a majestic 23-m (75-ft) pyramid. The pillars and the walls of the portico are decorated with stuccoed heads and hieroglyphics.

From the centre of the shrine, a stairway, which was originally blocked, leads to a crypt where Kin Pakal was buried. This is one of the few examples of a tomb enclosed within a pyramid. Although most of the excavated objects have been sent to the museum in Mexico City, the sarcophagus, covered by an enormous carved slab, is still in place.

The palace

Opposite the temple, the palace incorporates many patios and various constructions including an astounding four-storey tower, the only one of its kind: perhaps an observatory. Note the stucco figures and the fine bas-reliefs.

On the other side of the Río Otolum, the Temple of the Sun, the Temple of the Cross and the Temple of the Leafy Cross (Cruz Foliada), built under Chan-Balum's rule, have attractive carved reliefs. To the north is a group of five other buildings and a ball court.

Agua Azul

In the vicinity of Palenque, the waterfalls of Misol-Ha, 35 m (114 ft) high, and particularly those of Agua Azul, so-called because of the turquoise reflections of the water, provide spectacular settings for a pleasant picnic.

On the road to San Cristóbal, the site of Tonina, now engulfed by the jungle, was probably a major Maya ceremonial centre.

5

THE FIVE MOST INTERESTING MARKETS

The Indian *tianguis* are a veritable institution. Near Mexico City, don't miss the market at **Toluca**. In the Valley of Oaxaca, the Friday market at **Ocatlán** and Sunday's at **Tlacolula** date from pre-Hispanic times. In Chiapas, the daily (except Sundays) market at **San Cristóbal de las Casas** is visited by Indians from all the surrounding villages. Finally, a visit to **San Juan Chamula** market makes for a memorable excursion into Tzotzil country.

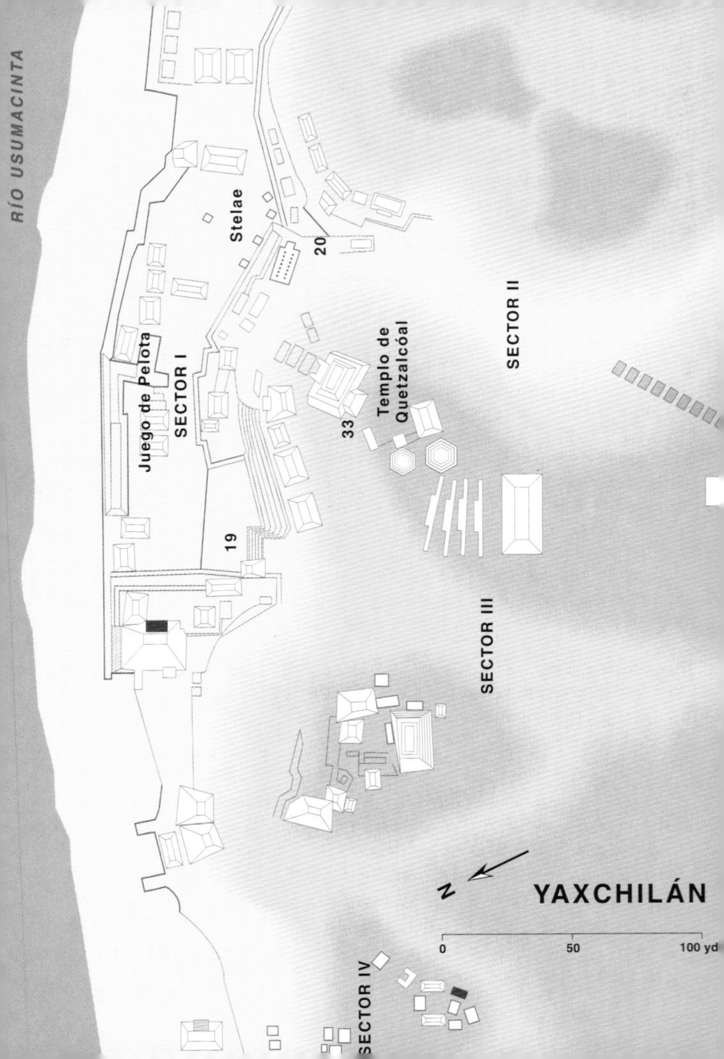

YAXCHILÁN

RÍO USUMACINTA
Juego de Pelota
SECTOR I
19
Stelae
20
33
Templo de Quetzalcóal
SECTOR II
SECTOR III
SECTOR IV
N
0
50
100 yd

The rushing waters of Agua Azul in Chiapas.

Yaxchilán

Located on the banks of the Usumacinta river, at a point where it is 200 m (656 ft) wide, the city of Yaxchilán is one of the most grandiose of the Maya sites. It is accessible only by plane, by four-wheel-drive vehicles or a journey upriver. In the heart of the virgin forest, it has the eerie atmosphere of a lost world. Larger than Palenque, it reached its golden age around the 8th century, under the reign of Shield of the Jaguar. The name means "place of the green stones".

The excavated buildings are grouped around a wide esplanade decorated with stone crocodiles and jaguars. By the river is a well-preserved ball court. Structure no. 20 has beautiful stelae. To the southeast, the pyramid (no. 33) has been blanketed by vegetation to become a hill. At its top is a temple, a shrine containing the statue of a jaguar-bird.

Bonampak

Only discovered after World War II, the ruins of Bonampak, fairly close to Yaxchitlán, are famous for their frescoes, a veritable almanac of Maya customs. The colours have faded, but the museum in Mexico City has copies showing their original appearance.

YUCATÁN

Campeche, Puuc Country, Mérida, Chichén Itzá, Cancún and the Caribbean Coast, Cobá, Chetumal

The peninsula of Yucatán juts out from eastern Mexico like the figurehead of a ship. The flat countryside of brush and sisal serve to emphasize the underlying generosity of the region. It combines all the ingredients of Mexico: from idyllic coastlines to submerged natural wonders, from straw huts to the elegance of colonial cities, from the pastel-painted houses of its inhabitants to the equally colourful cemeteries, and above all the unmistakable stamp of the Maya in the great cities of the ancient past.

Campeche

It was here, on March 20, 1517, that the conquistadors first set foot on Mexican soil. Twenty-three years later, under the leadership of Francisco de Montejo, they made the village of Ah Kim Pech their capital, setting out from here to conquer the rest of the Yucatán. Thanks to its prime position, on the west side of the peninsula, the sheltered village soon grew into a major port, attaining prosperity as the principal point for export of high-quality timber and dyewood, from which was extracted a prized red dye. Its rich cargoes tempted the pirates established on Isla del Carmen; in 1663 they plundered Campeche and massacred part of the population. Afterwards the town was fortified down to the channel leading to the port. It continued to prosper until independence was declared when it lost its statute of international port. As the modern capital of Campeche State, it has conserved a nostalgic charm.

The heart of town beats around the Zócalo and Alameda park, where entire families come for their evening promenade. The ramparts have been partially demolished, and only a fort and seven *baluartes*, or bastions, survive. Facing the park next to the cathedral, the bastion of La Soledad—the biggest of all—has been transformed into a museum displaying Maya stelae, and a small collection of weapons. There is a pleasant botanical garden at the Baluarte de Santiago, to the northeast; that of San Carlos, to the southwest, contains a museum of scale models. The regional museum on Calle 59 is housed in the 17th-century Casa del Teniente del Rey. It has fascinating polychrome statuettes from the island of Jaina, representing all the personalities of Maya society.

The typical Puuc style displayed in an arch at Labná.

Surrounded by a moat, San Miguel Fort, 4 km (3 miles) from the centre, houses the collections of the Archaeological Museum, including Olmec and Maya pieces.

Edzná

The small city is the main *Chenes* site. Derived from the Yucatec Mayan word for "well", the Chenes architectural style is particular to the southwest of Yucatán, and is characterized by a rich working of the stone and representations of Chac, the rain god.

Edzná is still partially concealed by the thick undergrowth, but on the edge of its plaza there is an impressive five-tiered pyramid, 30 m (98 ft) high.

Puuc Country

In the northwest of Yucatán, the Puuc country (*puuc* meaning "hill") is dotted with cities built in a characteristic style that evolved from the Chenes style during the post-classic period. The Puuc people, living in a region where water is scarce, considered Chac to be their principal god, and dedicated to him many ornamental elements in mosaics and geometric patterns. The buildings are constructed on a horizontal plan, particularly in the numerous palaces.

Uxmal

The origins of Uxmal are uncertain. Probably founded by Maya from Petén, it prospered from the 7th to the end of the 9th century, when it dominated the neighbouring cities of Kabah, Sayil, Xlapak and Labná.

Facing the entrance to the site, the oval-shaped Pyramid of the Soothsayer (Adivino) is an astonishing patchwork of Chene, Puuc and even Toltec influences. From the western façade, the view takes in the entire archaeological site, huddled together in a wide valley. At your feet, the Quadrángulo de Las Monjas (the Nuns), so-named for the cells arranged around a central court in the manner of a Christian cloister, was probably a royal college or a military academy. On the four buildings bordering the quadrangle you will notice numerous masks of Chac, as well as two feathered serpents (western building) imported from the Altiplano.

Leaving from the southern portico, you find yourself facing the ball court and beyond, an a large raised esplanade, is the superb Palace of the Governor, 120 m (393 ft) long. Typical of the Puuc style, the façade is very simple in the lower part, but extremely intricate in the higher sections. The Casa de las Tortugas is named after its frieze of tortoises, an animal associated with Chac.

The great pyramid adjoining the palace, restored on its northern face, rises to 30 m (98 ft). There is a magnificent view from the top. To the left is the Palomar ("dovecote" or "pigeon house"), an unusual structure of stone pierced by a lattice of holes. Its purpose is unknown. Every evening, ancient Uxmal springs back to life with a sound and light display around the quadrangle.

Kabah

Kabah is known for its Palace of Masks (Codz Po'op), covered with nearly 300 images of Chac. Unusually for the Puuc region, the sculptures start from the base of the building. You can also see a small pyramid, a palace, the Temple of the Columns and, on the other side of the road, an arch and several dilapidated structures.

Sayil

Near Kabah, the site boasts a monumental terraced three-storey palace, 85 m (93 yd) from end to end. It is a fine specimen of puuc design, alternating masks of Chac and sculpted columns. A few hundred yards away you can see the remains of the El Mirador temple.

The small settlement of Xlapak, 6 km (4 miles) east of Sayil, has several buildings in puuc style, but only one small palace has been restored.

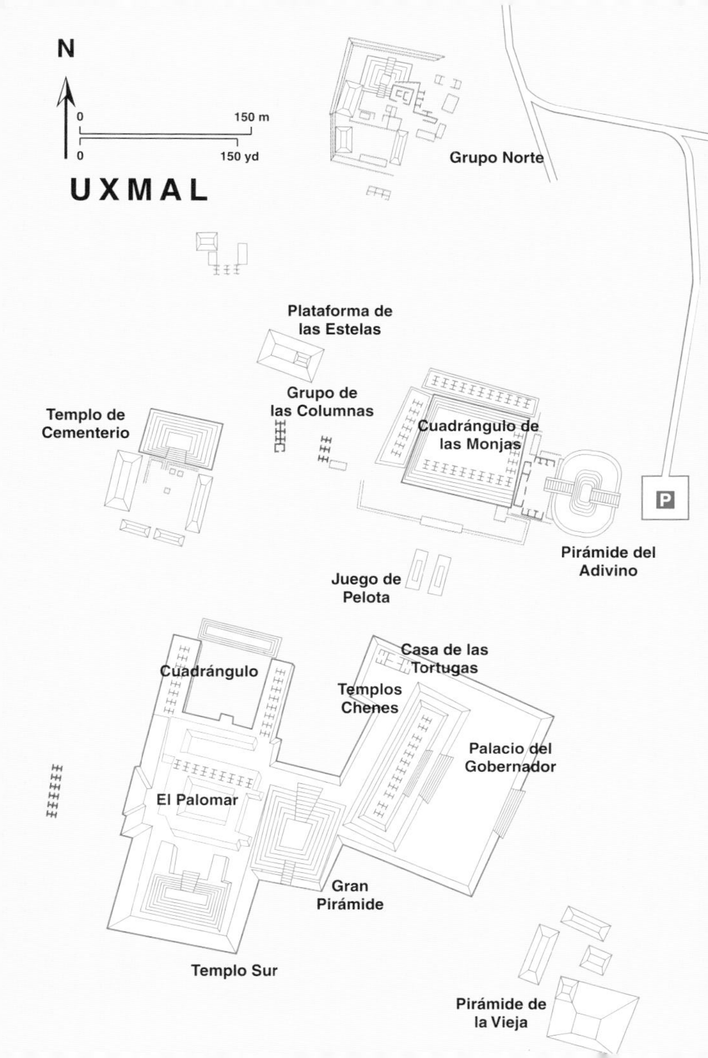
N
0
150 m
0
150 yd
UXMAL
Grupo Norte
Plataforma de las Estelas
Grupo de las Columnas
Templo de Cementerio
Cuadrángulo de las Monjas
Pirámide del Adivino
P
Juego de Pelota
Casa de las Tortugas
Cuadrángulo
Templos Chenes
Palacio del Gobernador
El Palomar
Gran Pirámide
Templo Sur
Pirámide de la Vieja

A beach for dreamers at Celestún, a birdwatcher's paradise.

Labná

The palace is adorned with the sculpture of a snake holding a human head in its mouth. A *sacbé* (causeway) leads to the little Pyramid of El Mirador and a very graceful arch, which is all that remains of another ancient building, 3 m (10 ft) high and 6 m (20 ft) long. The wings and façade are covered in Puuc motifs.

To the north, the Loltún caves have not only stalactites and stalagmites but also pre-Columbian paintings on the walls.

Mérida

An attractive colonial city of nonchalant charm, the capital of the Yucatán has drawn from its proud Maya and Spanish heritage a determination to conserve its importance.

The city is organized around the Plaza Mayor according to a plan that dates back to its founding by Francisco de Montejo in 1542. The square boasts some of the city's most handsome buildings. The 16th-century cathedral stands on the site of the temple of Tihó, a city razed by the Spaniards. Facing it are the Palacio de Gobierno, the town hall and the Montejo Palace, a splendid plateresque residence which belonged to the estate of the conquistador until the 1970s.

Southeast of the square, crafts, fruit and vegetables can be purchased at the municipal market. The Indians from the surrounding area, dressed in embroidered *huipil* shirts, come here to sell their colourful harvest.

North of the Zócalo, Calle 60 skirts the shaded benches of Parque Hidalgo and the church of Jesús (1618) then stretches to the Teatro Peón Contreras, built by an Italian at the beginning of the 20th century during a boom in the sisal hemp fibre trade. Folkdance performances are staged here on Wednesday evenings.

Beyond the University and Parque Santa Lucía (serenades on Thursday evenings), the north of the city is neatly set out along a wide boulevard, the Paseo de Montejo.

The Palacio Cantón stands as a grandiose symbol of Mérida's self-confidence in the late 19th and early 20th century. It now contains the regional museum, covering the history of the Yucatán from its beginnings. The displays devoted to nearby sites give a good overview of some of the lesser-known ones, such as Dzibilchaltún and Mayapán.

Dzibilchaltún

On the way to the port of Progresso, in the north, you could make a short detour to the site of Dzibilchaltún. Though it is only of minor interest in itself, the place is of historic importance as it was one of the first Maya settlements, probably before the year 1000 BC. On the site you can see the temple of the Seven Dolls (Siete Muñecas), and a *cenote* (well) with crystal-clear water.

Progreso

One of the Yucatán's principal commercial ports, Progreso lies on the northwest side of the peninsula, along a gently sloping beach. There's nothing spectacular about it, but thousands of city-dwellers from Mérida flock there at weekends and during holidays. Once they have all gone, the little town drifts back into its tropical slumber.

Celestún

Almost 100 km (60 miles) west of Mérida, the fishing village of Celestún is renowned for its lagoon, a national park where one of the continent's largest colonies of pink flamingos gathers every winter. See them up close on a morning boat trip, in the colourful company of pelicans, herons, anhingas and cormorants.

Further north along the coast, another fishing village, Sisal, is named for the fibre which was exported in great quantities in the early 20th century. The sisal boom fizzled out long ago, and the town now seems lost in time.

Chichén Itzá

Chichén Itzá is possibly the most fascinating testimonial of Mexico's pre-Columbian past, for its wealth of architectural treasures and the ambition of its conception. Moreover, two of the great civilizations of Meso-America—Maya and Toltec—are represented.

History

The story of Chichén Itzá begins at the end of the classical era, when it was probably founded by Maya settlers from Petén. Abandoned at an uncertain date and for unknown reasons, it was repopulated at the beginning of the second millennium after a Toltec invasion. Various myths back this theory: one story goes that it was under the king Ce Acatl Quetzalcoátl (also known as Topiltzín), exiled from Tula, that the city was resettled. Here, the feathered serpent became Kukulkán, and the fusion of the two cultures sparked a Yucatec renewal.

The Castillo

The visit starts in the northern part of the archaeological zone, which is the most recent. The principal structures, of Toltec influence, and exceptionally well restored, surround a wide esplanade. The nine-storey Castillo, or Pyramid of Kukulkán, rises majestically over 25 m (82 ft). Four stairways, one on each face, lead to the top, which is crowned by a temple. The head of an awe-inspiring stone serpent guards the foot of the northern face. During the spring and autumn equinox, due to the position of the pyramid's blocks, the image of a slithering snake seems to ripple along behind the head just as the sun sets.

Full of surprises, the building conceals another pyramid within. A dark, narrow underground passage leads to the site of the temple where archaeologists discovered a *chac-mool* and a throne in the shape of a jaguar.

The Esplanade

West of the pyramid, the largest of the eight ball courts, 135 m (442 ft) in length, is adorned with beautiful bas-reliefs, the best-known of which shows a player being beheaded. The Templo de los Tigres (of the Jaguars) next to it is decorated with friezes of felines. In front, the *tzompantli*, typically Toltec, is a wall carved with skulls, upon which the real skulls of sacrificial victims were displayed. A path takes you past the Casa de las Aguilas—where

Top: a reclining Chac-mool in Cancún; bottom: carving in the ball court at Chichén Itzá shows a player losing his head.

Edificio de las Monjas
Anexo Este
La Iglesia
El Caracol
Tumba del Gran Sacerdote
Akab-Dzib
Cenote de Xtoloc
Juego de Pelota
El Mercado
CHICHÉN ITZÁ
Juego de Pelota

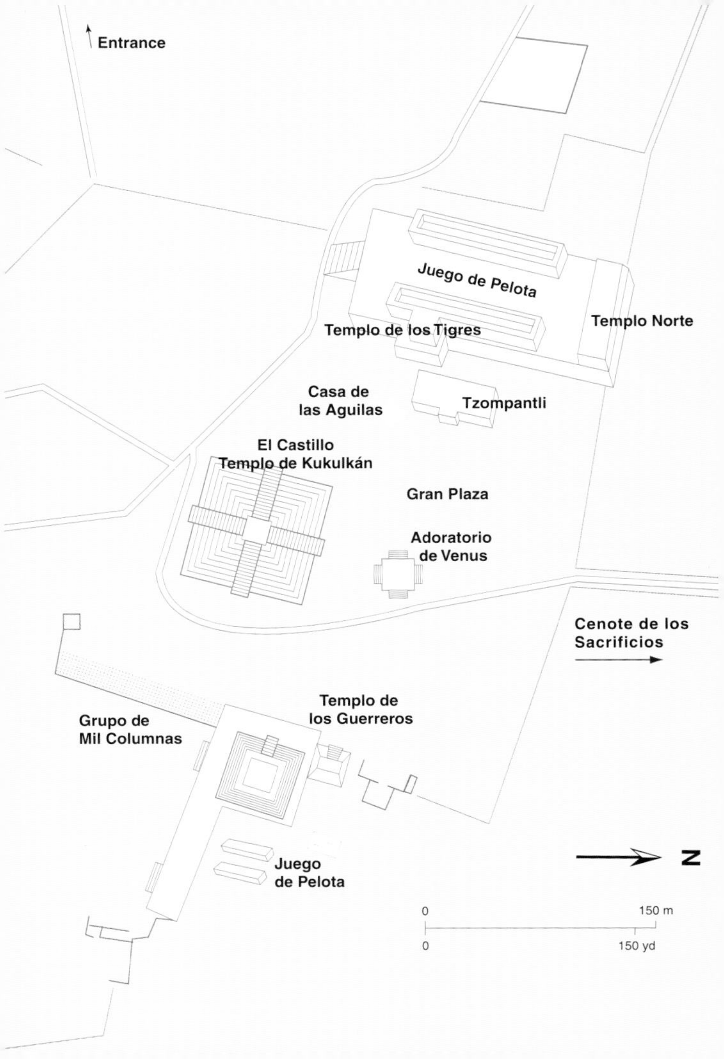
Entrance
Juego de Pelota
Templo Norte
Templo de los Tigres
Casa de
las Aguilas
Tzompantli
El Castillo
Templo de Kukulkán
Gran Plaza
Adoratorio
de Venus
Cenote de los
Sacrificios
Templo de
los Guerreros
Grupo de
Mil Columnas
Juego
de Pelota
N
0
150 m
0
150 yd

carved eagles are shown devouring human hearts—and the Temple of Venus, to the holy *cenote*. This large natural well, 60 m (196 ft) wide and 30 m (98 ft) deep, occasionally served as a sacrificial area. Archaeologists have recovered some forty skeletons and numerous offerings to Chac.

The Thousand Columns

To the east of the great pyramid, the complex of the Thousand Columns contains dozens of pillars (the remains of a covered building), the ruins of a steam bath and the Temple of the Warriors, of Toltec inspiration. On the upper platform reclines a *chacmool*, where human offerings were deposited, and further back is a table supported by carved male figures.

Southern Section

The Caracol, a round observatory, is the most interesting monument in this part of the site. At the top of the spiral stairway, seven windows are carefully aligned to precise points of the compass, probably having served to determine the date of the equinoxes, solstices and ritual ceremonies.

Next to the Caracol, you can see the building of the Nuns (Las Monjas) and its annex, together with La Iglesia, "the church", all in Puuc style.

Cancún and the Caribbean Coast

On the east of the Yucatán peninsula the state of Quintana Roo, for years the most impoverished in Mexico, has been transformed into a seaside Eldorado. Activities are centred around Cancún, but the fine sandy beaches stretch to the south as far as the marvellous Maya city of Tulum.

Cancún occupies a narrow strip of land shaped like the figure 7. The shore is lined with a string of luxury hotels rising between the white sands and swaying coconut palms. It's hard to believe that when the site of Cancún was chosen in 1969 after exhaustive research, only a handful of people lived here. Today this mega-resort rivals Acapulco, welcoming more than 3 million holidaymakers a year.

Cancún is known for its "air-conditioned" beaches—cool even when the sun is at its hottest. Needless to say, lounging on the beach is one of the main activities, but the clear waters are hard to resist, and when you've had enough of swimming and diving, you can also go deep-sea fishing. Or water-skiing and windsurfing on the Nichupté lagoon.

As for entertainment, each hotel has its own discotheque to liven the evenings, unless you prefer to watch a regional folk dance or a bullfight.

CANCÚN
N
0
3 km
0
1,5 miles
Laguna Chakmochuk
Punta Sam
Puerto Juárez
Jungla de Yucatán
Calle 48
Francisco I. Madero
Av. Uxmal
Av. Palenque
Av. Bonampak
Carlos J. Nader
Av. Tulum
Av. López Portillo
Av. Cobá
Av. Xcaret
Blvd. Kabah
Paseo Kukulcán
Mérida
Parque Aviario
Av. del Bosque
Av. del Bosque
Av. Sayil
Plaza de Toros
Av. Amigo
Av. Tulum
Jungla de Yucatán
Alfredo V. Bonfil
Av. Tulum
Paseo Kukulcán
Tulum
CANCÚN CENTRE
Av. Uxmal
Terminal de Autobuses
Monumento Historia del México
Av. Sunyaxchen
Iglesia de Cristo Rey
Monumento a Benito Juárez
Parque las Palmas
Av. Yaxchilán
Pal. de Gobierno
Palacio Municipal
Av. Tulum
Av. J.C. Nader
Av. Cobá
Av. Cobá
Av. Cobá
Parque Aviario
Av. Xcaret
Bahía de Mujeres
Playa Linda
Playa Langosta
Plaza Turquesa
Playa Tortugas
Centro de Convenciones
Museo Arqueológico
Campo de Golfo Pok-ta-Pok
Laguna Bojórquez
Isla Dorada
Mercado Plaza Flamingo
Yamil Lu'um
Playa Marlin
Laguna de Nichupté
Laguna del Armor
Cancún Queen
Mercado Plaza Cancún
Aquaworld
Playa Ballenas
Caribbea Sea
Campo de Golfo Caesar Park
San Miguelito
Laguna Cabra
Ruinas El Rey
Playa Delfines
Paseo Kukulcán
Laguna Río Inglés
Isla Paraíso
Parque Nacional Submarino Punta Nizuc
Punta Nizuc
180
307
307

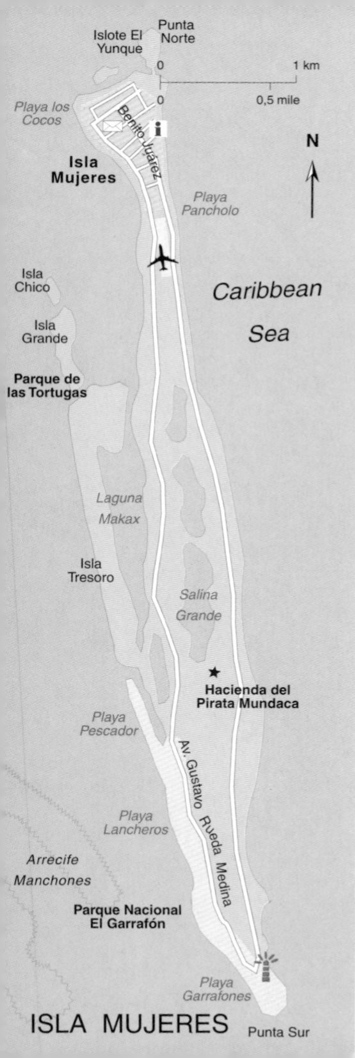

Isla Mujeres

A short distance off Cancún, the Island of Women used to be bypassed by tourists, but now it has developed into a pleasant and unpretentious beach resort. The island is only 8 km (5 miles) long and at most 800 m (876 yd) wide. It boasts fantastic beaches, especially on the western side (beware of strong currents on the eastern shore). Among the best are Playa Cocoteros, north of the resort, and Playa El Garrafón, today a national park on account of the beauty of its ocean floor.

At the southern tip of the island are the extremely dilapidated ruins of a Mayan temple dedicated to Ixchel, the moon goddess.

From Isla Mujeres, a 2-hour boat excursion takes you to the bird sanctuary of Isla Contoy.

Isla Holbox

Off the beaten track, the large Holbox island floats just off Yucatán's north coast, where the Caribbean Sea meets the Gulf of Mexico. Silt-laden waters lap the gently sloping beaches, spangled at low tide with millions of seashells carried by the waves. The time is long past when the island's natural harbour was the refuge of pirates. The inhabitants were once referred to as *selvajes* (sauvages) by the mainlanders; they still have the heritage of a turbulent past running through their veins.

Cozumel

Lying 20 km (12 miles) off the Yucatec coast, the large island of Cozumel is a favourite among divers. The bay of Chankanab, recently designated a national park, is a lagoon teeming with fish that are not at all bashful. For the true *aficionado*, the Palancar reef is a must: the coral formations are exceptional, and there is visibility up to 70 m (230 ft). There are many Maya remains scattered around the island, but most are in poor condition.

Riviera Maya

Over 100 km (60 miles) south from Cancún, the Caribbean laps exquisite stretches of light-coloured sand.

The first beach is also one of the most appealing: Playa del Carmen. This small fishing village has undergone unprecedented development, and a multitude of hotels and restaurants have been built to accommodate tourists. The beach is fantastic, lapped by turquoise waters that rival any Pacific paradise.

Following the coast, either north or south, other magnificent beaches unfurl, fringed by palm trees, each one more tranquil than the last. The diving is splendid, as is the fishing. Despite its expansion, Playa has not lost anything of its typical Yucatec atmosphere. As evening falls, the men mend their nets by the Zócalo, and as soon as it gets dark, the mariachis take up their well-known refrains.

Further south, Xcaret, a former Maya port, has been developed around the ruins into an "eco-archaeological park". Promoted as Nature's Sacred Paradise, it offers two underground rivers, a botanical garden, aviary, a "Maya Village", museum, restaurants and shops, not to mention countless activities such as swimming with dolphins, snorkelling, balloon rides, sea-walking and horse riding. Entertainment includes nightly folklore shows.

Xel-Há, another port of call for the Maya traders, close to Tulum, has been developed in a similar way, with the emphasis placed on ecology.

Tulum

This is the only Maya ceremonial centre that overlooks the sea, and its splendid setting makes up for the relative modesty of the buildings. In all likelihood it was built around 1200, and Tulum was still inhabited when the first Spanish ships sailed across from Europe.

Enclosed by a high, thick wall, the city bears witness to the wars between the city states at the end of the post-classic period. The well-preserved Temple of the

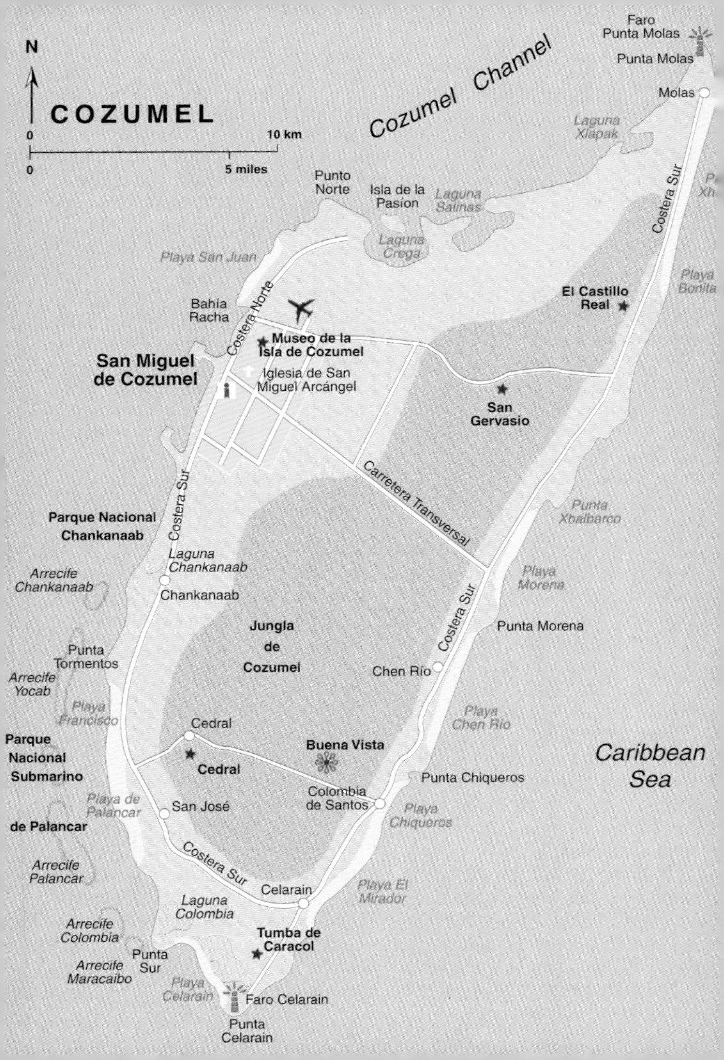
COZUMEL
N
0
10 km
0
5 miles
Cozumel Channel
Faro
Punta Molas
Punta Molas
Molas
Laguna
Xlapak
Costera Sur
Punto
Norte
Isla de la
Pasíon
Laguna
Salinas
Laguna
Crega
Playa San Juan
Playa
Bonita
El Castillo
Real
Bahía
Racha
Costera Norte
Museo de la
Isla de Cozumel
San Miguel
de Cozumel
Iglesia de San
Miguel Arcángel
San
Gervasio
Carretera Transversal
Costera Sur
Parque Nacional
Chankanaab
Punta
Xbalbarco
Laguna
Chankanaab
Arrecife
Chankanaab
Chankanaab
Playa
Morena
Costera Sur
Punta Morena
Jungla
de
Cozumel
Punta
Tormentos
Arrecife
Yocab
Chen Río
Playa
Francisco
Playa
Chen Río
Cedral
Parque
Nacional
Submarino
de Palancar
Buena Vista
Cedral
Caribbean
Sea
Punta Chiqueros
Playa de
Palancar
San José
Colombia
de Santos
Playa
Chiqueros
Costera Sur
Arrecife
Palancar
Celarain
Playa El
Mirador
Laguna
Colombia
Arrecife
Colombia
Tumba de
Caracol
Arrecife
Maracaibo
Punta
Sur
Playa
Celarain
Faro Celarain
Punta
Celarain

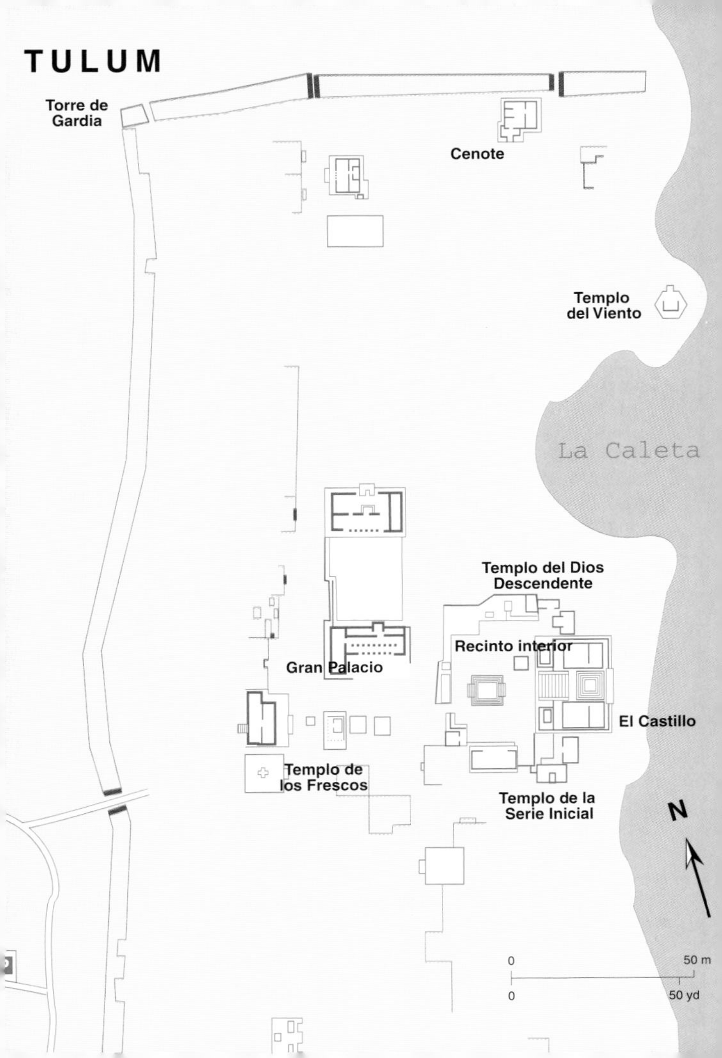
TULUM
Torre de Gardia
Cenote
Templo del Viento
La Caleta
Templo del Dios Descendente
Recinto interior
Gran Palacio
El Castillo
Templo de los Frescos
Templo de la Serie Inicial
N
0
50 m
0
50 yd

Frescoes has remains of mural paintings. To the north stands the main palace. On the edge of the cliff, the Castillo, comprising the temples of the Initial Series and of the Descending God, is Tulum's most imposing monument. It probably served as a watchtower. From the temple, the view takes in the entire site and the little beach of La Caleta, washed by the Caribbean surf.

Cobá

In the heart of the virgin forest, surrounded by numerous lakes, Cobá was a major Maya centre between the 7th and 9th centuries. Its architecture indicates strong ties with far-off Tikal, in Petén. The city is set at the centre of a network of *sacbeob*, wide, straight causeways, the longest stretching 100 km (60 miles).

Only 5 per cent of the archaeological zone has been excavated, and a visit combines the pleasure of discovery with the magic of a lost city. The Cobá Group stands out for its pyramid, 24 m (78 ft) high, known as the "church". The steep Pyramid of Nohoch Mul, further north, is the tallest in the Yucatán at 42 m (137 ft). Nearby, beside the road, stele no. 20 represents a member of the aristocracy accompanied by several kneeling prisoners. Other stelae are to be found in the Ma Can Xoc Group.

Chetumal

In the southeast of the Yucatan peninsula, on the shores of the Caribbean, the town of Chetumal marks the frontier between Mexico and Belize, formerly the British Honduras which gained its independence in 1971. The capital of the State of Quintana Roo, which is unprepossessing apart from its Museo de la Cultura Maya, makes a good base for visiting the local sites.

Bacalar Lagoon

To the north of Chetumal, the lagoon stretches over some 40 km (25 miles) parallel to the shore. It is famous for its clear turquoise water and was once linked directly to the sea, which enabled Spanish galleons to be repaired there in relative security. It was for this reason that at Bacalar itself a fort was built to protect the ships from English pirates. It has now been restored and houses a small colonial museum, with a good view over the lagoon.

Cenote Azul, just south of Bacalar, in a lovely wooded setting, forms a deep natural pool of dark blue water.

Kohunlich

West of Chetumal, on the Chiapas road, there are several little-visited Maya sites scattered around a region covered by the

Two Yucatán ladies in all their finery.

northern end of the Petén forest. Dating from the pre-classic period, Kohunlich, about 70 km (43 miles) from the capital of Quintana Roo, is still hidden among the vegetation. The Pyramid of the Masks, its most imposing monument with a height of 14 m (46 ft), has been magnificently restored. As a number of shelters have been built to protect the monuments from the rain, it isn't possible to get a good view of the grand staircase. But you can see close-up two of the eight superb masks of the sun god, each 2 m (over 6 ft) high, that used to flank it. Their features are similar to those of Olmec statues.

Other Maya Sites

Further west you can see the remains of the grandiose Xpuhil, which reached its zenith at the same time as Tikal (8th century). Only the main structure, with three towers, has been cleared of its cloak of vegetation.

A few kilometres away stand the ruins of Becán and, close by, those of Chicanná. These last enclose a temple whose central door is shaped like the jaws of a feathered serpent, and a pyramid decorated with masks of Chac, from a later period.

Lost in the forest, further south, are several great Maya cities: Río Bec, Calakmul, and so on.

CULTURAL NOTES

All Saints' Day. On the night of 1–2 November, every cemetery in Mexico sparkles with lights for the Feast of the Dead. The deceased are invited to leave the cemetery for a few hours and return to their former homes, where their favourite food awaits them. Religion, pagan rites and sheer love of the fiesta combine in a celebration that is joyous rather than mournful. The Mexicans' familiarity with death is a direct legacy of the Aztecs: Coatlícue, goddess of death, was at the same time the deity of life and fecundity.

The following day there is feasting. A main feature at the family gatherings is the *calaveras*, sugar or chocolate skulls, enclosing a skeleton-shaped trinket. Children love the *panes de muertos*, sweets gruesomely decorated with shinbone designs. Troops of papier-maché skeletons are paraded through the streets.

Architecture. At the time of the conquest, the Spaniards brought with them the architectural styles then prevailing in Europe. Gothic architecture was the norm in the early 16th century, but it was soon superseded by Renaissance influences. In colonial Mexico, this developed as the plateresque style, with ornamentation resembling silver filigree, which explains its name (*plata* means silver in Spanish). Occasionally, Iberia's Moorish heritage shows up in the Mudejar-style buildings that seem so unexpected in this part of the world. Another key decorative element is the *azulejo*, or coloured tile.

At the beginning of the 17th century, the baroque style developed in Europe. At first it was relatively restrained, but it took on an unbridled flamboyance in the 18th century under the Spanish architect José Churriguera. Transported to the New World, the style evolved into the exuberant flurry of details that typifies the churriguresque style. It gave free rein to the imagination of Indian artisans, who responded with an abundance of polychrome stone carvings and sculptures in their churches.

Aztec gods. The Mexican pantheon is one of the most complex in the world. At the foundation are 72 gods, but taking into account various permutations, archaeologists have identified some 1,600 deities.

Aztec tradition held that the world had been destroyed four times. To create the sun and the moon of the fifth and last world, two gods committed suicide by casting themselves into the fire. In return for this sacrifice, men had to offer up that which is most precious to them: their heart and their blood.

Huitzilopochtli was the Aztecs' guardian god, represented in the form of a hummingbird. He sprang fully armed from the womb of Coatlícue, the earth goddess. The instigator of war, he came to embody the triumphant sun.

Tezcatlipoca, the "Smoking Mirror", was most likely another manifestation of Huitzilopochtli. A youthful god of war, he also represented justice. It was he who vanquished Quetzalcóatl and drove him from Tula, giving rise to the myth of the return of the Feathered Serpent.

In the later years of the Empire, Quetzalcóatl appears to have had a following among the wiser Aztecs who had begun to question the need for human sacrifices.

Finally Tláloc, god of rain and fertility, and a carry-over from the earlier civilization of Teotihuacán, occupied a central place beside Huitzilopochtli.

Cocoa. Trade in cocoa dates back to the earliest pre-Hispanic civilizations. Some archaeologists believe that it formed the basis of the wealth of the Mayan cities controlling its production. In the Yucatán, as also occurred later on the high plateau, cocoa beans served as money: four beans would buy a rabbit. *Xocolatl*, the recipe for which was sent to Europe by the conquistadors, was reserved in Aztec times for the emperor and his warriors. Drunk cold, chocolate was flavoured with honey and spices.

Corn. The corn, or maize, crop is to Mexico what rice is to China. Deified since the earliest days of its domestication (about 6000 BC), *Zea mays* is responsible for the development of civilization in Meso-America. According to one legend, it was discovered by the gods and used to create man. Today there are 42 strains of corn—black, red, yellow, white—and no less than 605 recognized ways of preparing it, including 116 recipes for the *tortilla*, the corn pancake that is the staple of the Mexican diet.

Dress. Fashioned from wool or *ixtle*, a cactus fibre, the Indian costumes of Mexico survived the Spanish conquest. They are still often woven and dyed by hand using traditional methods: the *cochinilla* beetle that lives off cactus plants furnishes the red dye, sea snails the purple, various plants the yellow and green, and so forth. Weaving follows pre-Columbian methods, using patterns that haven't changed in centuries.

Traditional garb includes the *huipil*, a sleeveless tunic; the *quechquemitl* and the *rebozo*, shawls of one or two pieces; the *enredo*, wrapped around as a skirt and held snug at the waist by the *faja*, a sort of sash; the *sarape*, the Mexican model of the poncho. Outstanding embroidery work, owing to its particular colours and patterns, identifies the different tribes. The designs, symbolizing men, animals, plants and mythical forms, correspond to an ancient cosmology.

Maya gods. Maya society was governed by religious belief; its leaders were apparently also its priests. Life was ruled by astrology and complex rituals (bloodletting, scarification, votive offerings), but human sacrifices were rare among the Maya. It was only in the post-classic period (in Chichen Itzá) that the offering of human victims became common practice.

The Maya universe had four directions, thirteen paradises, and nine hells, each allocated to a god. Heading the pantheon, Itzamná, variously identified as the supreme Creator or his son, embodied the sky, in association with Kinich Ahau (the sun), and Ixchel (the moon). According to tradition the latter invented the written word.

A farming people, the Maya also venerated Chac, the rain god, and Yum Kaax (or Ah Mun), who represented corn and plant life.

A fairly late arrival from the mythology of the high plateau, Kukulkán was a Mayan rendering of Quetzalcóatl, with whom he shared the role of civilizer.

Mural Art. Springing from the Revolution of 1910, the muralist movement is the best-known artistic manifestation of modern Mexico. Portraying the suffering and struggles of the people in monumental frescoes, it became the means by which to promote social justice and Indian identity, illustrating the evils of colonization. Diego Rivera, David Siqueiros and José Clemente Orozco were the foremost muralists.

Shopping

Mexican crafts provide an inexhaustible source of souvenirs. With a skill that often borders on genius, craftsmen make objects in which style and form are combined in accordance with traditions going back thousands of years.

Where to shop

The markets, with their riot of colour and noise, offer the opportunity to buy at the source. In San Cristóbal, Oaxaca, Toluca and even Cuetzalán, the stalls feature a wide range of local products. In the smaller villages, choice is of course more limited, although it is here that you will find the best craftsmen.

In Mexico, bargaining is the accepted practice. If haggling is not your cup of tea, you always have the option of buying in shops where fixed prices are displayed. At least you can check what is on offer and at what cost (always higher), and perhaps decide to go back to join the bargaining game. Bear in mind that the asking prices are generally fair and the vendors often impoverished; it's up to you to come to an arrangement that will satisfy both buyer and seller.

Wood

The region of Michoacán is one of the richest in carved wooden objects. In Pátzcuaro, you will find Viejitos dance masks and the wooden cutlery of Zirahuén. Nearby Uruapan is famous for its lacquerwork on cedar wood. In the state of Guerrero, the village of Olinalá makes *rayado* lacquerwork with grooved patterns. Paintings on *amatl* (tree bark), with colourful naive motifs, are a speciality of Xilitla (Guerrero).

Leather

Leather goods are of high quality and usually a good buy. The north and the Chiapas area are the two main centres for this speciality, which includes wallets, handbags, belts, *huaraches* (Indian sandals), shoes and, naturally, the famous Mexican boots.

Metalwork

Silver has been worked for generations in Taxco: from a cigarette holder to a full dinner service, this is a quality item. You will also find silver jewellery, sometimes set with turquoise, statuettes, vases, and original de-

signs combining metal and porcelain. In the Bajío, Guanajuato is known for its gold jewellery. Santa Clara del Cobre, in Michoacán, was once one of the principal copper mining centres in the country. The town still has several dozen workshops producing candlesticks, lamps and trays.

Pottery

Available in all shapes and sizes, pottery comes in essentially two styles: in unbaked clay, as in pre-Hispanic times, or baked and decorated, Spanish-style. This last is often glazed, in a multitude of bright colours or plain green. In Coyotepec (Oaxaca) items are moulded with the hands, without a potter's wheel. In Tonalá, near Guadalajara, ceramics are decorated with designs of flowers, animals, or landscapes.

The fascinating "trees of life" —resembling candelabra—have their origin in the pre-Columbian myths. The ones from the Mixtec village of Acatlán (Puebla) are specially prized. The main problem is getting them back home. You will also find animal-shaped figurines of black or painted clay.

Finally, why not take home a copy of a Maya or Aztec statue? If the quality of some efforts leaves much to be desired, others are so well crafted that occasionally they are passed off as the genuine article.

Clothing

Indian costumes—brightly coloured, hand-woven, embroidered with intricate symbols—are works of art. Obviously, the best place to shop for them is in the Indian states.

The most attractive embroidered *huipiles* are to be found in the Yucatán. The *rebozos* (stoles) and *sarapes* (ponchos), however, can be picked up almost anywhere, though the ones from Santa María del Río are said to be the most beautiful in the country. In the Oaxaca valley, Teotitlán is famous for its magnificent bedcovers with traditional or modern designs—details from Picasso paintings, for example.

Wickerwork

Wicker and straw are used not only to make baskets but also for hats: the northern-style *sombrero* (embroidered in gold or silver), the round, pointed headdress of the peasants of Cuernavaca (rare), or *jipijapa*, the Panama hat of Yucatán.

And also...

There's always room in a suitcase for a Yucatec cotton hammock: look for a *"matrimonial"* (double-sized) one, always more comfortable whether for one occupant or two.

Finally, the guitars from Paracho have a worldwide reputation.

Dining Out

Mexicans love eating. "The plaza and the restaurant are the two cornerstones of Mexican culture", author Carlos Fuentes once wrote.

The cuisine reflects the country's history. Its foundation is corn, a legacy of past civilizations which is prepared in hundreds of ways. The tortilla*, a thin pancake, was already enjoyed in Olmec times. Náhuatl, the language of the Aztecs, has given us among others the words* tomatl *(tomato),* cacahuaquahit *(cocoa), and* xocolatl *(chocolate).*

Timing

Traditionally, the midday *comida* is served between 1 and 4 p.m. Nevertheless many Mexican restaurants, accustomed to catering for foreign customers, are happy to adapt meal times according to demand.

Breakfast

Hotels tend to offer an American-style breakfast: eggs with bacon or ham, cereal, toast, fruit juice and coffee. Mexicans themselves usually settle for a simple *pan dulce*—a sweet bun—accompanied by weak tea or very strong coffee. If they are really hungry they'll order *huevos mexicanos* (scrambled eggs with tomato, onions and peppers) or *huevos motulenos* (a tortilla covered with ham, eggs, cheese and tomato sauce garnished with peas).

Snacks

The tortilla is the basis of nearly all the *antojitos*, literally "little fancies"—snacks that can be eaten at any time of day or night. Some of them amount to a meal in themselves. The famous *enchiladas* are tortillas fried and rolled up around a beef or chicken stuffing with beans and cheese, then baked and served in a spicy sauce. *Tacos* are small tortillas, again rolled around a stuffing and fastened with a toothpick; they can be eaten fried or unfried. *Tostadas* are tortillas that are fried until gold and crisp, then covered with meat, fish or chilli sauce. Yet another variety is the *quesadilla*, folded over the stuffing like a turnover and fried.

At the start of every meal, you will be offered a bowl of delicious creamy *guacamole*, an avo-

***Mexicans love to eat, and preferably* al fresco.**

cado purée seasoned with onions, tomato and lemon, to be scooped up with crispy tortilla triangles or used as a sauce.

Also common are *tamales*, made from a more elaborate dough, stuffed with meat, beans and peppers, wrapped in corn husks and steamed.

Meat

Few Mexican dishes come without chilli peppers or at least a chilli sauce. Beware if you are not accustomed to spicy food. The green ones are generally hotter than the red. The hottest *chiles*, grown in the Puebla region, are the *habanero* and *serrano*. *Chiles rellenos* are bell peppers stuffed with minced meat, almonds or cheese and deep-fried in an egg batter.

Mole poblano can be considered the national dish of Mexico. Meaning "puebla sauce", it is in fact turkey (or chicken) accompanied by a sauce made with chillis, herbs and spices, and chocolate. It can take several days to prepare. Chicken can also be served *pibil* style (cooked in a banana leaf). The same dish, with duck, is *pipan de pato*.

The beef is excellent. Everywhere there are places specializing in grilled meat *(carne asada)*, called *tebone* in the north. Beef that is dried *(machada)* or dried and then cooked *(cecina)* are specialities of the north.

Fish and Shellfish

Pompano blanco with green sauce, using the white fish of Lake Pátzcuaro, is praised as the best fish dish in Mexico. Veracruz-style red snapper *(huachinango)* is another delicacy, garnished with onions, peppers, tomatoes and saffron sauce, and sometimes stuffed with scallops. The very popular *ceviche* is raw fish marinated in lemon juice to "cook" it, mixed with chopped onions, peppers, garlic and tomatoes. Shellfish, especially lobster, is to be found in all the beach resorts.

Only order fish near the coast or lake where it was caught.

Specialities

Certain pre-Columbian dishes have survived the centuries and are still enjoyed today. Among the more unusual delicacies: grilled grasshoppers; *gusanos de maguey* (agave caterpillars), grilled and served with guacamole; *escamoles*, the larvae of red ants served with green sauce or lemon; snake. But the best-known culinary curiosity is without doubt the *ahuautli*, the Aztec version of caviar: mosquito larvae, a famous though rare treat, available only in summer. *Nopal* (the young, fleshy paddles of the prickly pear cactus) are a traditional peasant dish. They are sometimes served in a salad.

Desserts

It is said that there are at least 1,000 different types of dessert in Mexico, but it is in the *dulcería* (sweet pastries) that you will find the greatest selection. Otherwise, caramel custard, rice pudding, cakes and ice cream are the most usual offerings, without forgetting the luscious exotic fruits: guavas, papaws (papaya), pineapples, bananas, mangoes, custard apples or sugared sapodilla berries.

Beverages

Tap water is generally suspect: stick to bottled mineral water, and avoid ice cubes of unknown origin. Corner stands sell cold fruit juices in addition to the more familiar soft drinks.

Tequila, *mezcal* and *pulque*—all made from the agave—are the national drinks of Mexico. Only the milky *pulque* is produced by fermentation alone; the others are distilled. The popular Margarita is a cocktail of tequila, orange liqueur and lime juice.

Mexico produces numerous beers (more than 25 brands, most of them lager-type) and, in Baja California and the Bajío, wine of reasonable quality.

Sports

With 10,000 km (6,200 miles) of coastline, Mexico is a paradise for water sports, and the varied landscape in the country's interior allows numerous outdoors activities.

Mexicans themselves are more interested in spectator sports: they are passionate about beisbol *(baseball), wrestling, bullfighting, football (soccer), jai alai, and rodeos, seen live or broadcast on television.*

By the Sea

Mexico's shores are washed by some of the most beautiful waters in the world, the Pacific Ocean and the Caribbean Sea. Long, sandy beaches are an open invitation to enjoy all sorts of leisure activities. The water is almost always warm, and swimming is a delight.

On most beaches, you can go windsurfing, water-skiing, parasailing, jet-skiing or you can rent a boat, canoe or kayak. Serious surfers will find waves to be reckoned with in Baja California, Ixtapa and Puerto Escondido.

Deep-sea fishing is practised all along the Pacific coast, especially off Acapulco, Zihuatanejo, Puerto Vallarta (with its famous swordfishing competition) and Baja California.

Scuba diving is especially good on the Caribbean coast. The Palancár Reef off the island of Cozumel, with good visibility down to 70 m (230 ft), attracts divers from all over the world. If you prefer snorkelling, explore the lagoons of Yal-Ku and Xel-Ha, which are teeming with tropical fish. On the Pacific coast, Puerto Vallarta National Park is also renowned: you can spot dolphins, whales and manta rays, look into underwater caves and along the reefs, in shark-free waters.

On Land

Wherever the land meets the sea, you can hire horses for an exhilarating gallop along the shore, or go on an inland trek.

Every big resort—and many towns—have at least one golf course open to visitors.

Tennis is played all over the country, on public courts or those belonging to hotels. It's best to time your game for the cooler

Ixtapa is a paradise for surfers, fishermen and golfers.

hours of the morning, to avoid the worst of the midday heat.

In the Mountains

The trend of hiking and rock-climbing has reached Mexico, via the US. The ascent of Mount Popocatépetl (5,452 m/17,900 ft), was extremely popular, and considered to be fairly easy. With a departure before sunrise, it could be climbed in a day. However, since the volcano erupted in 1997, it has been out of bounds. Should the ban have been lifted by the time you get to Mexico, bear in mind that you shouldn't try this if you have no experience of trekking through snow, or if you are not in good physical condition. You should also be aware of the risk of altitude sickness, one reason why the ascent of Iztaccíhuatl (5,286 m/17,340 ft) is reserved for seasoned mountaineers.

Another fashionable destination for outdoor types, the Barranca del Cobre in the heart of Tarahumara territory, offers a different experience altogether. Setting out from Creel or Batopilas, you plunge into the bowels of the canyon (12-hour round-trip), or you can spend more days exploring the Sierra, journeying from one gorge to another, from one village to the next.

The Hard Facts

To plan your trip, here are some of the practical details you should know about Mexico:

Airports
Most international flights land at Benito Juárez Airport, 15 km (9 miles) south of Mexico City. Its modern terminal has restaurants, shops, post office, currency exchange offices, car hire agencies (Hall E) and tourist information office (Hall A).

If you need a taxi, you must purchase a ticket at the office in the airport (official rate). Bus service links the airport and the capital every 15 minutes between 6 a.m. and 10 p.m. The Aeropuerto Metro station, on the Observatorio-Pantitlán line, is 20 minutes' walking distance from the airport.

The Miguel Hidalgo Airport in Guadalajara (domestic and international flights) is 20 km (12 miles) southeast of the city. There is a coach service every 10 minutes from 5 a.m. to midnight.

General Juan N. Alvarez Airport, 26 km (16 miles) southeast of Acapulco, has direct connections with some European cities. A coach service transfers passengers to the city centre in one hour. If you take a taxi, agree on the fare in advance. You can also share a limousine with four other passengers.

A number of other regional airports have direct air connections with US destinations.

Climate
Mexico is in the northern hemisphere and the seasons are, in theory at least, the same as in Europe: hot in summer, cold in winter, when there may be frost or even snow on the plateaux. At this latitude the rainy season, from the end of May to September, should be taken into account, though rainstorms are generally short. Winter is by and large the best time to visit. The varied topography, which accounts for a great range of microclimates, enables you to enjoy the beach any time of year.

Communications
Stamps are sold at the post office *(Correos)* and at the hotel reception desk. Letters can take one to two weeks (sometimes more for postcards). If you wish to send a telegram, head for the *oficina de*

telégrafos, but be warned, even these can take several days to reach their destination. It's fairly easy to send a fax from major post offices; otherwise the hotel will send your fax for a fee.

To phone abroad, you can call from your hotel or from a Ladatel phone booth *(larga distancia)*. You will find these in larger towns, airports, railway stations and some bus stations. Instructions for use are shown in three languages, including English. Dial 98 (international service), then your country code (44 for the UK, 1 for the US and Canada, 353 for Ireland, 61 for Australia), followed by the area code (minus the initial zero) and local number. Some phone booths accept only coins, so have a good supply handy. Others take phone cards, which can be purchased at TELEMEX offices, or even credit cards. Note that phone charges are very high. Reduced rates for calls to Europe apply all day at weekends and on weekdays from 6 p.m. to 6 a.m.

Consulates

All foreign embassies are located in Mexico City, but many countries also have consular representation in other large cities. In case of a major mishap (loss of important documents, trouble with local authorities) do not hesitate to contact them.

Crime

In spite of its bad reputation, Mexico is not an exceptionally dangerous country for travellers. Theft is generally limited to pickpockets who prowl crowded places. To reduce risks, deposit your valuables and documents in the hotel safe.

In seaside resorts (the Oaxaca coast in particular), avoid walking on the beach after dark. And do not leave anything in sight inside a parked car.

Currency

The currency is the Nuevo Peso (N$), divided into 100 centavos (¢). Coins range from 5¢ to N$10; banknotes from N$10 to N$100.

Traveller's cheques in US dollars can be exchanged at almost any bank; those in European currencies are more difficult to cash. It is easy to withdraw cash with your Visa or MasterCard at banks or automatic cash points if you remember your PIN. Credit cards are widely accepted.

Driving

Mexico's roads are fairly good. Speed limit is normally 80 kph (50 mph), 100 kph (60 mph) on highways and 110 kph (68 mph) on motorways. A common hazard is the tendency of animals to wander onto the roadside or even into the middle of the road.

Be wary of the *topes*, countless "sleeping policemen" or speed bumps (rarely signposted) located at the entrance and exit of the smallest hamlet. Keep an eye out for traffic lights, frequently located at the opposite side of crossroads. In general, it is best to avoid driving at night.

There is no shortage of service stations, and petrol is inexpensive, although unleaded petrol is sometimes more difficult to find. If your car breaks down, do not despair: the main roads are patrolled by teams of Angeles Verdes (Green Angels), who provide mechanical assistance free of charge, courtesy of Mexico's tourist authorities.

Driving in cities, especially Mexico City, is a nightmare of constant traffic jams, pollution and fruitless searches for a parking space (the tow-away trucks are very efficient). It is best to get around by public transport.

Essentials

Should you forget to pack something, do not worry: you will find all you need at your destination. Nevertheless, if you are using medication, bring these with you: brand names and dosage may differ in Mexico.

For clothing, you should allow for a bit of everything: lightweight clothes for the coast, warmer clothing for regions situated at higher altitudes. Don't forget that Mexico City is at a height of 2,240 m (7,350 ft). A raincoat could come in handy in summer.

Formalities

Visitors from most countries, including the UK, Ireland and Australia, require a valid passport and a tourist card *(tarjeta de turista)*, valid for up to 90 days. The latter can be obtained at Mexican consulates abroad or from your airline. US, Canadian and Japanese citizens may enter with a birth certificate or other national ID and a tourist card.

Health

Medical facilities in the larger cities are reliable, but in smaller villages this is not always the case. Rural hospitals can treat a cut or offer advice if you come down with a case of "Montezuma's Revenge", but in more serious medical emergencies it is best to go elsewhere. Consider taking out medical insurance covering repatriation in case of illness, before your visit.

There are some common-sense precautions you should take: drink plenty of liquids to prevent dehydration, but avoid tap water, and beware of the mosquitoes (you'll bless the day you packed an insecticide in your travelling kit). No special vaccinations are required for visiting Mexico.

Vaccinations against typhoid and hepatitis are a good idea, especially if you intend to travel in tropical regions. Some visitors also choose to take preventive treatment against malaria (Chiapas, Tabasco).

Holidays and Festivals

There are countless fiestas, but most are celebrated at a local level. Nationwide, the public administration offices and some shops close on the following dates:

January 1	*Año Nuevo*
February 5	*Aniversario de la Constitución*
March 21	*Nacimiento de Benito Juárez*
March/April	*Pascua/Semana Santa*
May 1	*Día del Trabajo*
May 5	*Batalla de Puebla*
September 1	*Informa presidencial*
September 16	*Día de la Independencia*
October 12	*Día de la Raza* (Columbus Day)
November 1–2	*Día de los Muertos*
November 20	*Aniversario de la Revolución*
December 12	*Nuestra Señora de Guadalupe*
December 25	*Navidad*

Language

Spanish is Mexico's only official language, spoken by most of the population. English is widely spoken in the major destinations, especially in large cities and in hotels, but Mexicans, fiercely loyal to their cultural identity, prefer to be addressed in Spanish. Try to learn just a few words to break the ice. Coming out with English you risk being branded a Gringo—and the price of purchases can rise accordingly. You'll find a list of handy phrases at the beginning of this guide.

Media

Mexico has a range of local and national periodicals. The most widely read newspapers are *El Tiempo* and *Excelsior*. In Mexico City and in tourist destinations there are also newspapers and magazines published in English.

Aside from Mexican television, which broadcasts in Spanish only, many hotels offer satellite broadcasts, mainly American programmes.

Opening Hours

Banks keep relatively short hours, generally 9 a.m. to 1.30 p.m. on weekdays.

Most shops and public offices are open from around 9 a.m., taking a long midday break for lunch and the *siesta* to reopen from around 4 p.m. to 7 or 8 p.m.

Museum opening hours vary, but are usually 9 or 10 a.m. to 5 or 6 p.m. Shorter opening hours are kept on Sundays and holidays. Most museums are closed on Monday.

Archaeological sites are open daily from 8 or 9 a.m. to 5 or 6 p.m. Check in advance whether there are special restricted hours for visiting tombs or the interior chambers of pyramids.

Photography

You can find practically all types of film on sale in photography shops, hotels (where they are more expensive) and chemists. Colour film is the most common. Prices tend to be lower than in Europe, but before you buy, make sure to check the expiry date on the box.

Time

Mexico straddles three different time zones. Most of the country is located in the Central Time Zone (the same as US Central Standard Time), GMT –6 in winter, and GMT –5 in summer. This means that all year round, when it is noon in Mexico City, it is 6 p.m. in London.

The northwest states fall within the Mountain Time Zone, one hour behind Mexico City, and Baja California is in the Pacific Time Zone, two hours behind the capital.

Tipping

The *propina* is, like in Europe, left to the discretion of the customer. Nevertheless, in resorts patronized by Americans your waiter will expect a tip amounting to 15 or 20% of the bill.

Toilets

You will find public toilets in airports, train stations, roadside rest stops, museums, etc., but do not expect miracles as regards the facilities. The best bet is to use the toilets at hotels. To use the facilities in a café, it is advisable to order a drink as well.

Tourist Information

The Mexican Tourism Ministry maintains a network of visitor information offices at the more popular destinations. It also has a toll-free telephone information service in English and Spanish: dial (01 5) 525 93 80.

In Mexico City and in each state, local authorities offer their own services, often very efficient.

Transport

Between cities, the airplane is the best way to travel. Airlines serve even the smaller country towns.

The railway network, although fairly extensive, is of limited interest: trains are slow and punctuality is virtually non-existent.

Coach travel, which is inexpensive, will take you to the furthest corners of the country. Service is frequent and reasonably comfortable if you travel on a first-class coach, though some routes seem to take forever.

For short distances, or for a journey lasting several weeks, hiring a car will give you freedom of movement. The minimum age for renting a car is usually 25, although some firms will hire to those aged 21 and over. North American and European driving licenses are accepted. Rates are comparable to those of western Europe (and you will save money if you reserve before your visit).

In cities, taxis are numerous and reasonable, but make sure that the meter is working, or arrange the fare in advance. The city bus routes wind endlessly through the outskirts. In Mexico City, they stop only at designated stops, but the *colectivos* (minibuses) stop wherever the passenger requests.

Another option in Mexico City is the Metro, practical and well organized. Avoid using it during rush hour.

Voltage

Electricity is supplied at 110 volts, 60 cycles. Plugs are the American-style ones, with two flat prongs. Europeans travelling with their hair driers, personal computers, etc. should pack a plug adaptor and a transformer.

INDEX

ABCs OF ANCIENT MEXICO

Cenote Natural wells of the Yucatán, used as a sacrificial site by the Maya.

Chac-mool Messenger of the gods, a deity represented reclining on his back, legs bent.

Chinampa Floating man-made garden on a lagoon in the Mexico Basin.

Codex Illuminated parchment.

Copal Resin used an incense.

Glyphe A written symbol used by the Maya.

Mexicas The Aztec name for themselves.

Popol Vuh Book of the Sacred Council of the Quiché Maya.

Puuc Hilly region around Mérida.

Sacbé Maya man-made causeway of unknown purpose.

Tlachtli Ball game, in Náhuatl.

Tzompantli Wall of Skulls, where the skulls of victims sacrificed to the Sun were displayed.

GENERAL EDITOR:
Barbara Ender-Jones
ENGLISH ADAPTATION:
Mark Little
LAYOUT:
Luc Malherbe
PHOTO CREDITS:
Hémisphères back cover, pp. 44, 50, 61, 66, 79, 84, 87, 91, 96, 98 (top), 114, 120;
Claude-Hervé Bazin pp. 4, 13, 16, 21, 30, 35, 56, 63, 93, 98 (bottom), 117;
Mireille Vautier pp. 1, 6, 26, 72, 80, 109
MAPS:
JPM Publications
Elsner & Schichor
Huber Kartographie

12, avenue William-Fraisse,
1006 Lausanne, Switzerland
information@jpmguides.com
www.jpmguides.com/

Printed in Switzerland
Gessler/Sion (CTF)